Lost Ancient Technology

Of Peru And Bolivia

Copyright Brien Foerster 2012

All photos in this book other than those taken by the author are assumed to be copyright free; obtained from internet free file sharing sites.

Table Of Contents

1/ Introduction

2/ Sachsayhuaman

3/ Qenqo

4/ Amaru Machay

5/ Coricancha

6/ Inca Roca Wall

7/ Pisaq

8/ Naupa Iglesia

9/ Ollantaytambo

10/ Machu Picchu

11/ Inti Punku

12/ Temple Of Viracocha

13/ Pucara

14/ Sillustani

15/ Chucuito

16/ Amaru Muru

17/ Tiwanaku And Puma Punku

18/ El Fuerte De Samaipata

19/ Quillarumiyoq

20/ Saihuite

21/ Vilcashuaman

22/ Intihuasi

23/ Huaytara

24/ Huanuco Pampa

25/ Chavin De Huantar

26/ Cumbemayo

27/ Conclusions

28/ Bibliography

1/ Introduction

Exploring a secret cave in Peru with the brilliant Christopher Dunn

When one thinks of Peru, in a historical context, the names that immediately spring to mind are the Inca, and the Spanish Conquistadors; that is, if any knowledge of this South American nation is known at all. The Inca were the largest civilization of the pre-Columbian Americas, and the Conquistadors were a small group of Spanish soldiers of fortune who utterly decimated these proud and advanced people beginning in 1532, under the leadership of Francisco Pizarro. The details of how the "conquest" by this group of 160 odd Europeans of the great Inca was conducted and achieved is accounted in my book **A Brief History Of The Incas: From Rise, Through Reign To Ruin**, available as a print book from

www.adventuresunlimitedpress.com as well as many bookstores in Peru, including on top of Machu Picchu. It can also be purchased as an e-book from **www.hiddenincatours.com** and **www.amazon.com**, along with my other Inca related books and others.

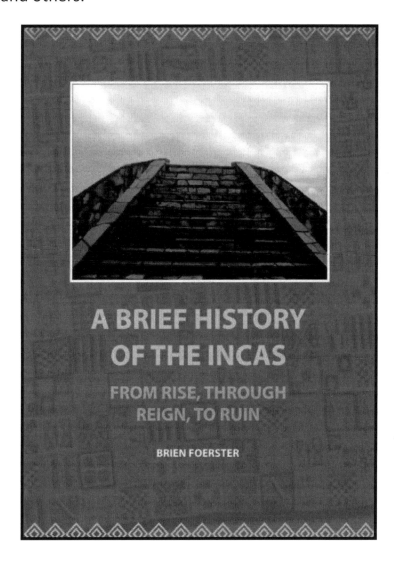

The sole purpose, if one reads all of the Spanish accounts and oral traditions of the Inca descendants of the "conquest" was to obtain by any means the vast wealth of the Inca, mainly gold but also silver which Pizarro and his motley group of Spanish misfits had heard rumours of while they were in Panama, years before. Local Panamanian natives could not help but notice the Europeans', and especially Pizarro's obsession with the gold amulets and nuggets that adorned some of the indigenous peoples' necks, and one chief is said to have expressed that if the Spanish were so hungry for this metal, they should go to a place called Pelu, south and west of Panama. He said that gold was so plentiful that the people ate from plates of the material, and drank from golden cups.

What few readers will know is that the first two of three attempts by Pizarro to find this mysterious, and what would turn out to be elusive (as written about in my aforementioned book) "Pelu" were not government sanctioned voyages, they were in fact the acts of very desperate men. Pizarro was born illegitimate, and was raised as a swine herd in a rural area of Castile, Spain. His aspirations were to leave his native land as soon as possible, and thus set out, as many did, for the so called "New World" where gold and other riches were said to be plentiful and easy to obtain.

The problem that he and others faced was how to pay for passage? As many if not most of the emigrants to the "New World" were at the bottom rung of the social classes, they had to barter their way across the Atlantic. Often they wrote, or at least signed (commonly with an X, being illiterate) a promissory note which clearly stated that they would repay a loan once they struck it rich in this mysterious and far off land of plenty. The problem was, to a great extent they were duped, because Panama had little to offer, aside from disease, heat, humidity and a desperate population of Native people who were waning due to previous European encounters.

Thus, the plight of Pizarro and many others was; return to Spain and debtor's prison, or do what ever it took to acquire wealth, and that meant literally anything. In general, it was not hard for Pizarro to rally a crew from amongst Panama's expatriate population. With promises of unbelievable wealth they set off, and on the third attempt landed on the shores of what is now called Peru, and the rest, as they say is history.

More pertinent to the topic of this book is what the Spanish (I will no longer use the term conquistador in this book, as it is fiction that there was any nobility, honour or ethics in any of their pursuits) encountered once they arrived in Cuzco, the Inca capital, having ravaged the local populations and their wealth all along the way from their first footsteps on the shore.

The chronicles written by the Spanish show that these Europeans were in awe and bewildered by some of the stone structures presumably built by the Inca and/or their ancestors. Massive constructions, such as the megalithic Sachsayhuaman above Cusco seemed inconceivable; how could these Natives have shaped and manipulated multi-ton blocks of hard stone, at least one of which weighed 125 tons? And perhaps even more impressive, no mortar or cement of any kind was evident, the stones appearing to, in some cases fit so well that a piece of paper could not fit between them?

In some of the "first contact" and colonial period writings, mainly penned by the Spanish, Inca descendants are said to have stated that some works, such as the great zig zag wall of Sachsayhuaman, which we shall discuss first, were made by ancient people, in fact giants. Whether "giants" referred to beings of great stature or immense intellect is uncertain. Also, one must take into account that the Spanish, from their first encounters with the Inca and other Native people in generally treated the Indigenous people of these lands with contempt, and the Europeans felt a sense of superiority.

This was shown by the banishment and wanton burning of the Inca khipu system of knotted cords, which clearly was not only a form of accounting, but indeed some surmise could have also been a form of recorded language. As well, temples, starting with the Inca "holiest of holies" the Coricancha in Cusco was town down to its foundations soon after the Spanish entered this Inca capital city, to be replaced by a Catholic church.

To systematically remove a peoples' belief system means to control not only their spirituality, but also their sense of self and identity, thus, one must consider that some of most of what the Inca descendants "taught" the Spanish invaders was not the reality of their history. Why would you tell an oppressor your most sacred information.

Though the Inca are now gone as a civilization and a people, and much of their history literally burnt in front of their eyes (as in the khipu) magnificent stone structures, built by them and those that preceded them remain, in abundance.

Much of the Inca city of Cusco was taken apart by the Spanish colonials in order to build their own structures. Many Inca period buildings were made up of andesite and basalt stone blocks approximately one cubic foot in size. Therefore, it was not only easy for the Europeans to take these walls apart in order to construct their own, but it saved them the time and effort of establishing and working their own quarries.

The megalithic walls were, I am sure left as a last resort for building materials. The sheer size, hardness, and location of many of the stones and structures meant that they would require incredible effort to break up, transport and shape. Luckily they still exist, somewhat bruised but not broken for us to examine and enjoy today. And kudos to the Peruvian Government for assisting in their preservation.

2/ Sachsayhuaman

Engineer Arlan Andrews inspecting an ancient shaped surface near Sachsayhuaman

Aside from the gold and silver that adorned the walls of temples, which they took with brute force of course, they visited a site above the city called Sachsayhuaman, which, depending on the source you consult either means "Head of the Puma", "Head of the Falcon" though the former carries more weight since it is well known, amongst the oral traditions of the Inca that the city of Cusco, prior to Spanish occupation in 1533 was formed in the shape of a puma, with Sachsayhuaman forming the head, in the north. A more recent meaning I have been told, through my friend who is a Native guide in the Cusco area, Rogelio

Gibaja Tapia for Sachsayhuaman is "head of completion" or "place of completion." This would be a spiritual name and understanding.

What astonished the Europeans, and does with visitors to this day was the size of the hewn stones that make up the first tier (of which there are three) of the zig zag wall and surroundings. The largest weighs upwards of 125 tons, and is almost 30 feet tall, 12 of those feet being buried in the ground and thus forming a very firm foundation, necessary to keep the wall stable as Cusco is a very seismically active area.

The author below the Puma paw section of Sachsayhuaman

It is and was not only the size of the stones, but the fact that they fit precisely together without any kind of mortar, and that each stone is unique in shape and volume; more complex than any that the Spanish had seen in their European homeland. How could "natives" have achieved what white God fearing Catholics had not was their question? The answers vary, depending what source you consult. As most of the Spanish chronicles of the time and soon after tend to have a racist tinge to them, and the most famous Inca account was written by the half Inca Garcilaso de la Vega, who left Peru in his early twenties and wrote his historical account in Spain under the watchful eye of church and state, one must sift carefully.

The zig zag wall of Sachsayhuaman and a curious stone in front

A common statement from the Inca sources of the time was that the megalithic aspects, such as the giant zig zag wall were built by "giants" prior to Inca occupation, which occurred around 1100 AD, and/or by the mysterious Viracochan people who had pre-existed the Inca. Inca construction did of course occur in the area, but as we shall see later on in the book, the scale and craftsmanship of the work does not compare with what I and others regard as the work of the far earlier and more superior "megalithic builders."

This is in no way meant to belittle or simplify the Inca and their accomplishments, but a careful look into the archaeological record clearly indicates that the tools found could not have shaped the stones, being of a hardness of 6 to 7 on the Mohs scale (10 being diamond.) Why is this? The Inca knew of metallurgy, obviously, because they worked gold and silver, which turned out to be their downfall at the hands of the Spanish. They also shaped tools, weapons and ornaments out of copper and copper alloys, such as bronze, which is abundant in the highlands of Peru, since the local Andes mountains are volcanic. Iron is present in the form of iron oxide, and is plentiful in the telltale red soil of the area, but there is little indication that the Inca were capable of smelting it.

Copper and bronze chisels are reasonably common in archaeological digs, but that material is so soft in comparison to the andesite, basalt and granite stones used in the ancient structures at Sachsayhuaman and around Cusco that one strike would take any cutting edge off the chisel, and repeated blows would simply bend it. Stone hammers were also employed, but in order to remove material in any kind of efficient way from the stone (andesite, basalt or granite) being shaped, the hammer would have to be harder.

Meteorite material tools as well as those of hematite and iron pyrite have been found, and average 6 on the Mohs scale (1) which is more or less, or even softer that the stone being shaped. These tools, no matter how many workers were employed and over how many generations most likely did not create the zig zag wall at Sachsayhuaman, and many other buildings, structures and shaped outcrops that we shall explore in the coming pages.

As stated, the Inca clearly built at the Sachsayhuaman site, but no historic accounts that I have found indicate how the giant stones which make up the giant wall were moved, shaped or fitted together. The quarry from which the stones were brought is estimated to be approximately 35 km away (2) but the question arises, how would anybody have moved them? The natural answer would be wooden rollers made from tree trunks, but prior to the arrival of eucyaluptus from Australia, specifically the Blue Gum variety in the latter half of the nineteenth century (3) there were no large straight native trees in abundance.

Western scholars who have attempted to explain how the stones were moved from the quarry, shaped and fitted into place have the following to say: 'The stones were rough-cut to the approximate shape in the quarries using river cobbles.' (4) What? 'They were then dragged by rope to the construction site, a feat that at times required hundreds of men.' (5) This quote was written in 1600, more than 60 years *after* the fall of the Inca. 'Cieza de León, who visited Sachsayhuaman two times in the late 1540's, mentions the quarrying of the stones, their transposition to the site, and the digging of foundation trenches. All this was conducted by rotational labour under the close supervision of Imperial architects.' (6) However, how could Cieza de Leon have witnessed the construction in the 1540's when the Inca fell in 1533?

I hope that what you are starting to see is that descriptions of the construction of such sites like Sachsayhuaman are in the realm of speculation *after the fact*. To add insult to injury, here is another: 'Vince Lee is an author, architect, and explorer who has studied and consulted on various ancient sites where people moved large megaliths. He theorized that the blocks at Sachsayhuaman were put into place by carving them and then lowering them into place. The stones would have been precisely carved in advance to create the tight joints made to fit into prepared pockets in the wall. Then the stones would be towed up a ramp and above the wall, where they would be placed on top of a stack of logs. The logs would be removed one at a time to lower the stones into place. In contrast Protzen, a professor of architecture, has shown, he says, how the Inca built long and complex ramps within the stone quarries near Ollantaytambo, and how additional ramps were built to drag the blocks to the construction above the village. He suggests that similar ramps would have been built at Sachsayhuaman. (7)

It is beyond being "unlikely" that the tools in the archaeological record could not have achieved what the above theories speculate upon; and thus it leaves the great zig zag wall of Sachsayhuaman a mystery to this day. But, it is only one of many amazing examples of what I regard as lost ancient technological accomplishments at Sachsayhuaman, not to mention the city of Qosqo (Cusco) and beyond for us to explore in this book.

Inca period tools in a museum in Cusco

Inca period constructions can clearly be seen if you walk up to the third tier of the zig zag wall. They are off to the western side. Recently this area has been cordoned off with ropes due to archaeological digs, but this may not be the case if and when you visit. What you will see are small blocks of stone, often two or three levels in height, and reasonably well shaped. The tell tale white dots on the stones indicate where stone Inca hammers have been used for the final finishing;

these are often called "bruise marks." If the Inca had shaped the giant megalithic stones of the zig zag wall these bruise marks would be all over the surface of each stone; but is not the case. Some bruising can be seen, but not in a consistent fashion.

The wall sections with the small stones is Inca, but not the rest

You will see a large circle of low lying stones. This shows you where a large tower once stood, torn down by the Spanish as well as all other Inca constructions in the area. The reason why the Spanish took the Inca buildings apart and not the massive zig zag wall, was because the stones of the Inca structures could be easily carried away, and tended to be cube shaped, and thus could be incorporated into colonial buildings, since Spanish masons were used to working with square shapes.

This was the case in Cusco itself, where the Inca period buildings, which tended to be made of stones small and squared off, or field stone could easily and quickly be used to construct walls, and since the Spanish knew how to use concrete, which the Inca did not. In fact, close inspection of the colonial buildings shows you that the Spanish masons sometimes used concrete mortar of more than an inch in between the set stones, and this accounts for their weakness when it comes to earthquakes, which are frequent in Cusco. The concrete is softer than the hard Andean stones, and thus crumbles during a tremor, while many of the Inca buildings were designed to withstand earthquakes, and the pre-Inca megalithic structures do not waver, and have not for thousands of years.

Proposed Inca stone work and later Spanish "repairs" using mortar

Following the siege of Cusco in 1556, when the puppet high Inca, called Manco Inca (set in place by Pizarro in order to appease the Native population) decided to burn Cusco to the ground from Sachsayhuaman by volleying flaming projectiles, the Spanish rebuilt the city. Sachsayhayhuaman and other sacred structures were destroyed block by block to build the new governmental and religious buildings of the city, as well as the houses of the wealthiest Spaniards. In the words of Garcilaso de la Vega, the half Inca writer, "to save themselves the expense, effort and delay with which the Indians worked the stone, they (conquistadors) pulled down all the smooth masonry in the walls. There is indeed not a house in the city that has not been made of this stone, or at least the houses built by the Spaniards." (8)

Sachsayhuaman is an enormous site, and much larger than the zig zag walls and structures that lie (or once did) on top of it. It spreads out to the north and east by probably hundreds of hectares; in fact, new archaeological studies keep extending its size, so no one really knows how large it is. When viewed from the southern and south western hills, one notices that the whole of the hill on which it rests, rising above Cusco, is terraced. But the terracing is so covered by foliage over the course of the last 500 years that stone walls, some being massive megalithic ones, may be yet to be unearthed.

The Cusco expert of the megalithic structures of Cusco and the Sacred Valley, Jesus Gamarra, whose father Alfredo preceded him, showed me the interior of a restaurant part way down the flank of Sachsayhuaman. Here we saw a truly mehgalithic wall, and Jesus insists that the entire hill is an ancient megalithic pyramid, capped by Sachsayhuaman, and far older than the Inca. More of his work and thoughts, as well as information about how to hire him as a guide can be found at: www.theorigintour.com

Traveling north from the zig-zag wall, and across the grass field where the yearly Inca "rebirth of the sun" spectacle called Inti Raymi is held on June 24, mainly for tourists but also a profound celebration of Inca majesty and culture, you will face a huge exposed bedrock mound, with stairs leading up onto it. This is where we find our next amazing example of lost ancient technology evidence. It is called Suchuna in Quechua, but I do not know what that means in English.

The average local tour guide will tell you, based on information indoctrinated into him or her from the western archaeological biased tourism school, that you are looking at thrones, used during Inca times by the high officials of the Inca civilization to observe festivals happening on the grassy plain you just walked across. The problem with this idea is that the "thrones" face west, while the grassy "parade ground" is to the south, causing the Inca to wrench their necks in order to observe the pageantry.

The Suchuna "observatory" at Sachsayhuaman

Far more logical is the idea that this was a calendar of some sort, either solar, lunar or both. Soltices and equinoxes seem to line up with the 13 steps there, and of course 13 is the number of moon cycles in a year. However, it is unlikely that the Inca shaped it. Again, the stone here is the ever present andesite, with hardness of 6 to 7 on the Mohs scale, and heavily layered with even harder quartz crystal. Did the Inca use it? Most likely, but did they shape it? Doubtful.

One thing to know and keep in mind is that the amazing megalithic structures in Cusco, the Sacred Valley of Peru and elsewhere are rarely in isolation. Where you find one you will often find others in close proximity, and this is perhaps especially true at Sachsayhuaman, Ollantaytambo in the Sacred Valley, and Machu Picchu.

Observations with Chris Dunn in August 2012: almost perfectly level

One thing I will also endeavour to do in this book is to call the structures we find by their Native Quechua names wherever possible, and basically refuse to use any Spanish ones, as they are often tainted by Catholic influence. The original names of the megalithic places will most likely never be known, so the Inca ones will be the best that we can find. In some instances the English will have to be used, for those places to which I don't yet know their Quechua names.

One case in point is a rarely (thankfully off the worn tourist route) visited spot, still used today for ceremonies, called, in English, the Temple of the Rainbow. As the Spanish name translates as "the devil's door" you can see why I wrote the above rant. But more of that later…

Moving further north, beyond the 13 finely crafted "thrones" and following a trail slightly to the left we encounter a fine example of extremely ancient cut out flat and vertical surfaces, again referred to by local guides as yet more Inca "thrones."

Engineer Dan checks the flatness of services with me

This is called the Inca graveyard by most guides, which may be true. The area was only excavated in the 1990s I believe, and complete skeletons in the foetal position were found, but were they Inca? That is as yet unknown, as they have not been carbon 14 tested for age. What does make them intriguing however, is that some have elongated skulls, a subject covered in my book with David Hatcher Childress called **The Enigma Of Cranial Deformation; Elongated Skulls Of The**

Ancients, available through **www.adventuresunlimitedpress.com** and also **www.amazon.com**.

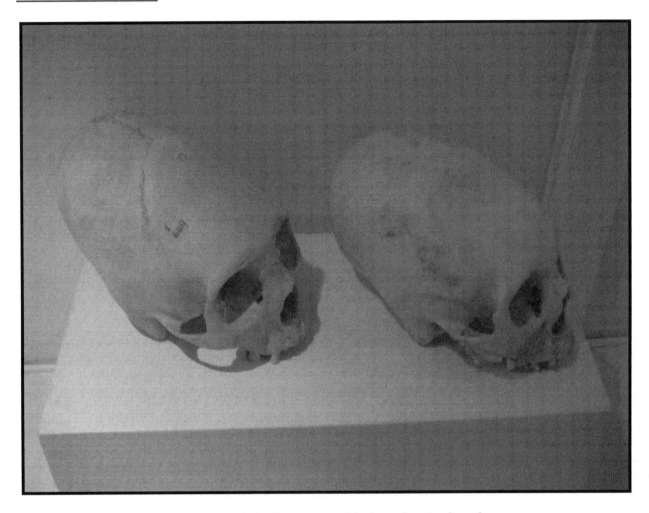

Two of the elongated skulls presumably found at Sachsayhuaman

This opens up a real can of worms, because elongated skulls, in my opinion and as continued research suggests, are associated with megalithic structures and these "Inca" may be the descendants of those that built the ancient things we are and will be looking at. The amount of erosion on the hard andesite stone, presumably from rainfall would indicate that much more than 500 or so years have passed since these surfaces were shaped, and there is no evidence of tool marks.

One stone, seemingly snapped into three gigantic sections is especially intriguing, not only because it appears to have been snapped by some gigantic catastrophe, but also because it appears to be upside down. This may indicate, though not yet proven, that the violent upheavals that seemingly occurred somewhere in the region of 12,000 years ago, resulting in the ending of the last ice age, melting of the ice sheets and causing a global rise of the oceans by approximate 350 feet, could have caused this. And this could add to the evidence that we are exploring here.

The seemingly "flipped over staircase" at Sachsayhuaman

Beyond this area you will see a large circle, also towards the north. This is usually explained as having been a ceremonial place, which is probably the most over-used term used in Cusco and the area, aside from the dreaded other one, "sacred space" or "place of meditation." These terms are used when the guides and or archaeologists can't come up with a more authentic and coherent explanation, and why I consult people with knowledge of oral traditions to illuminate me.

If you truly spend time looking at this circle, you will see that there were far more stone rows in place prior, one would guess to the Spanish invasion. The stones still there, which are quite close fitting are of the size the Spanish would have prized for their own building purposes, and thus took them away to Cusco. Oral traditions, thanks to knowledgeable experts like Jesus Gamarra and Jesus Merello state that during Inca times this circle was a reflecting pool, filled with water in order to study celestial bodies. Evidence supporting this idea you will find if you walk to the east inside the circle. Once you get to a solid bedrock wall, an opening will appear before you. This is in fact a tunnel, which you can walk through, bent over. As it could easily have carried water, it may have been the drain for the giant reflecting pool. As for where the water came from, Cusco gets lots of rain, and the Inca were masters of water diversion, mainly for agricultural purposes, but also pools.

Part of the stone wall of the "circle" area showing two different construction styles

Since the western area has been massively altered since Inca times, no signs of the water entrance remain, but the circle is a very damp place during the rainy season of November through March.

One of the most intriguing, and seldom explored places is next, and again you must walk north along the trail. After a few hundred meters you will see a massive boulder, as large as a house in front of you. Closer inspection that literally the entire surface, on the sides and top have been sculpted, again, not likely by the Inca, but a far older culture. This is called the Chinkana stone.

The amazing Chinkana stone

The mysterious process used to remove cube like pieces of andesite from the bedrock you will also have seen at the "Inca graveyard" and is described by Jesus Gamarra as having been done, based on his father Alfredo's theory, by the Hanan Pacha, or first culture. Although I do not agree with some of the details of the explanations of the Gamarras, or their time lines which are based on the bible, I definitely give credence to their basic hypothesis. That is that three cultures existed in the Cusco area, and beyond.

The first, or as they call it Hanan Pacha culture were those responsible with shaping the bedrock, removing the cube like chunks, and were also the makers of structures which were constructed from unique polygonal blocks, such as the zig-zag wall of Sachsayhuaman, as well as some others we shall encounter on this journey. The second, which they term Uran Pacha were a later second culture, who made the super tight fitting walls of more regular sized stones. A prime example of this we will see at the Coricancha, which was the spiritual center of the Inca, and lies more or less in the heart of central Inca Cusco.

Detail of sculpted andesite surfaces of the Chinkana stone

The third culture, called by the Gamarras Ukan Pacha, include the Inca, as well as the Huari (or Wari) who were the dominant people of the Peruvian highlands prior to the rise of the Inca. Their workmanship is far more inferior to the two earlier cultures, and could have been achieved with bronze chisels and stone hammers, the earlier ones? No way.

Out of respect to the Gamarras, I wish to use their terminology, and any mislabelling of the structures henceforth are completely my fault, not theirs. The Hanan of Hanan Pacha in simple terms refers to the highest of three worlds and levels of consciousness in the Inca frame of mind, and is represented by the Condor bird. The Uran Pacha is the middle world and refers to the mid level of consciouness, who animal representation is that of the Puma cat, and the Ukan Pacha is the lower world, whose symbol is the Serpent, called Amaru in Quechua.

Condor, our English word is derived from the Quechua Kuntur, and Puma is also a Quechua word. Also, Pacha means earth or world. The most popular use of Pacha today is the term Pachamama, which means mother earth, and one of the most famous of the high Inca, the one who expanded the Inca world, called the Tawantinsuyu (4 sections of the Inca world) was Pachacutec. His name in English translates roughly as the "Earth Shaker" or "one Who Turns Over The World."

This also coincides with the Quechua term Pachacuti, which is a cycle of time, being 500 years, and means "When The World Turns Over." This is in reference to the Inca way of looking at cycles of time, a dark period of 500 years is followed by a period of light. The last Pachacuti was 1992, when we entered the period of light. The previous one was 1492...need I say more?

Anyway, around to the east side of the stone a large slab has broken off, and is said to cover an ancient staircase which leads down to a tunnel. This is not here say or myth, a gentleman whose daughter owns a restaurant that I frequent in Cusco worked for the archaeology department of Peru, Previously called the INC and now the Ministry of Culture, and he helped excavate and clean up many of the ancient sites around Cusco and the Sacred Valley. It is statement, and those of others, that he personally climbed down the staircase prior to 1992, when the government sealed it off. He descended down 60 meters and was met with a labyrinth of tunnels, high enough to walk through upright.

The main tunnel leads 2 km south, to the Coricancha, which I mentioned briefly before. I t has been said by eye witnesses that the exit point of the tunnel is below the Coricancha, but the Catholic church, who now owns the Coricancha and has done for almost 500 years prohibit anyone from entering it? Why? Because it is dark, splits off into sub tunnels, and you would get lost. The name for tunnel in Quechua (Runa Simi) is Chinkana, hence the nearby stone has the same name due to its proximity.

Snapped off staircase of the Chinkana stone, clearly from a cataclysmic event

There is much more to explore in the Sachsayhuaman archaeological site, but as far as I can tell I have covered the main points for you here. Now we move north east, and follow the main southern, and quite modern road towards the Sacred Valley. This asphalt highway is right on top of a major Inca trail, and is possibly far older than that culture.

Small sculpted and shaped stone structures appear to the left and right of the road, with still under excavation. What you will notice is that Hanan Pacha forms the base, with later Uran Pacha blending in, and in some cases, the Inca Ukan

Pacha. This is a phenomenon we will see time and again, the Inca seemingly did not interfere or alter the works of the two older cultures, but harmoniously added on to what existed before.

Other oddities at Sachsayhuaman

3/ Qenqo

And now, on the right, and less than a kilometre away is a massive andesite outcrop, similar to what we saw at the Chinkana, but far larger and more complex. This is called Qenqo, or sometimes written as Kenqo or even Kenko, which means, "zig zag," referring to a carved area, no longer open to visitors, which is shaped like a, well, zig zag. A the bottom of it is a small pool, smaller than a dinner plate. Most guides will tell you that the Inca poured either Chicha, which is corn beer into the top of the zig zag or perhaps the blood of a slaughtered Llama. More zealous guides will say human blood was used, which is nonsense. The path and rate that the liquid made supposedly was used by the Inca to foretell future events, such as crop yields.

Strange intentional rounded cut marks on a stone at Qenqo

But Qenqo is far more complex and older than being a site of Inca ceremony. Upon entering the site via the conventional tourist route, in front of the massive carved bedrock megalith stands a large stone, about 4 meters tall. Most of the local guides call it either a puma or frog figure, but a lack of defined carving of the surface, even taking into account possible thousands of years of erosion make it, does not convince me that it is more than natural.

Entrance to the Qenqo passageway, or labyrinth

What is intriguing is that this stone is surrounded by a low wall, once higher but "quarried" yet again by the Spanish, which seems to have been made by what the Gamarras would call the Uran Pacha culture. As you move to the right, and through a doorway that yet again was "harvested" by the Spanish, a passage greets you. This opening was clearly the work of nature, most likely not erosion but a catastrophic splitting of the massive stone and subsidence, which was later shaped using some type of technology.

Hanan Pacha workmanship seems to be here, in the form of indentations in the wall, but like much of this ancient and mysterious culture's work, the reasoning for such "creases" is illusive. Upon departing from the other end of the passage, you will look upon more striking Hanan Pacha work, all around you.

Turning to the right and moving down a few old steps, a second passage shows itself, this one being more of a tunnel about 30 to 40 meters long. Again, it is a natural entry, yet has amazing examples of Hanan Pacha, including a sculpted table of sorts. This, according to most tour guides, was a ceremonial altar used by the Inca for the mummification of the Inca royalty. The cool and natural climate of the cave would allow for the slow and careful drying of the corpse, and with the addition of herbs such as Muna, which is a very fragrant herb, preservation would be complete.

All of the chronicles that I have read speak of the fact that the high ruling Inca, called Sapa, were so adored that they were preserved through deliberate mummification. Ancestor veneration frightened the Spanish crown and clergy, who destroyed the burial chambers, or huacas, of these corpses in an attempt to undermine the ancestral foundation of the Incan empire. (9) And it is said that the 12 great ruling Sapa Inca, from the founder Manco Capac to Huayna Capac were preserved and kept up to the time of the Spanish conquest, where they were either secreted away by the remaining Inca in caves, as yet still not found, or burned by the Spanish.

As with most ancient sites in the area, Qenqo was of course used by the Inca, and their presence can be seen in the addition of their constructions to those of the older cultures. A split in the ceiling of the cave, presumably the result of earthquake or other catastrophic activity could have either proceeded, or preceded the interior shaping of the surfaces, hard to tell.

The proposed Inca "ceremonial altar"

Exit from the interior of the huge Qenqo stone

4/ Amaru Machay

Our next site is about a half hour walk from Qenqo, to the northeast, and is, again, a large and natural andesite outcropping with the Hanan Pacha sculpted surfaces, as well as those features we have seen of the later two cultures. This is known in English as the Temple of the Moon, and in Quechua as Amaru Machay, which means the "cave of the serpent." It in fact has two caves, that of the sun, which you will see first, and of the moon second.

These names and depictions fit in with the Inca concept of duality, where the sun, Inti in Quechua is the male aspect and the moon, Quilla, or Killa, the feminine. What the original shapers, the Hanan Pacha called them we have no clue, as their sole memory is that left in their stone work. Could they have been people with elongated skulls, like those or related to those we find buried close and at megalithic sites, and of which the Inca may have been the descendants? Or was the devastation caused by the presumed catastrophe that ended the ice age so extensive, in this area at least, that no sign of them is left?

Entrance to the "Sun Cave" at Amaru Machay

One problem we have with the archaeological record is that they seem to have a preconceived notion that the earliest culture in the Cusco area, prior to the Inca, were the Killka. The Killke occupied the region from 900 to 1200, prior to the arrival of the Inca. Carbon 14 dating of Sacsayhuaman, had demonstrated that the Killke culture constructed the fortress about 1100. The Inca later expanded and occupied the complex in the 13th century and after. (10)

However, if the excavations were to proceed much deeper, evidence of earlier cultures could be present. Such is the nature of archaeology that the deeper you dig, the further back in time you go, generally. However, exceptions do occur, such as what we shall see when we explore Tiwanaku and Puma Punku later in the book.

Inside the "Moon Cave" at Amaru Machay

The interior of both the sun and moon caves are clear examples of Hanan Pacha, and show evidence of polished andesite surfaces. Whether the shine is the result of the stone having been hand worked or vitrified by heat or some other agent will require analysis of the possible layers of the stone in a laboratory, which to my knowledge has not been done. What we will see later on are whether stone, such as granite and andesite, which are igneous or metamorphic have examples where the surface has sloughed off. That is more a feature of sedimentary rock.

This could provide us evidence of heat or some other force altering the surface of the stone, causing it to separate from that which is found deeper inside.

Highly polished or maybe vitrified stone at Amaru Machay

There are many more examples of ancient Hanan Pacha structures, with the later Uran and Ukan Pacha additions in the area, especially if you travel north along a still used Inca trail. This trail in fact leads into the Sacred Valley eventually. Showing photos and descriptions of them in total would make this book much larger than necessary, and according to Jesus Gamarra, there are 5000 Hanan Pacha structures in the Cusco and Sacred Valley area!

Two more sites of interest in this area take us yet further north, and afterwards we will retreat back south to explore Cusco itself, and then beyond. Puca Puccara, meaning red fort in Quechua was an Inca fort, used to control entry and exit to Cusco from the Sacred Valley. The Inca were incredibly intelligent and organized when it came to social order and organization, and master tax collectors. The Inca road system was to some degree inherited from earlier cultures, such as the Huari, and greatly improved and expanded by the Inca. As you shall see later on, I suggest that the main arteries were in fact made by the master megalithic builders. Under the Inca, trade and commerce, as well as the efficient movement of the military were the prime uses of the roads, and all civilians who wished to walk them needed to pay a tax, in the form of a percentage of the goods they were carrying.

We do find minor activity by the Hanan Pacha here, but not much; most of this site is of Inca design and execution. From here, to the northwest you can see our last stop along this route, Tambo Machay. This, during the time of the Inca was a sacred bathing place of the Inca nobles and the Virgins of the Sun, young women, brought from throughout the Inca world to prepare the food of the highest of the Inca, weave their garments from the rare and soft Vicuna wool (relative of the Lllama but not able to be domesticated) and tend to...other needs shall we say.

Tambo is the Quechua word for inn and/or storehouse, and Machay, as we have seen is cave. It is the movement of water here, more than the "cave aspect" which seems to have been of importance. The ritual bathing of the Inca and the Virgins of the Sun (Nuestra in Quechua) included prayer, and it was thought that the prayers of such high ranking people would energize the water, which was then directed towards the agricultural terraces. There are examples of Hanan Pacha and Uran Pacha here as well, mainly in the form of two fountains, so it shows us that the "Inca" road fro Sachsayhuaman to here, and probably beyond may be thousands of years older than the Inca. And now to Cusco...

Very fine masonry at Tambo Machay

The logical way to return to Cusco on this journey is not just to jump there, symbolically, but to return to Sachsayhuaman, and more specifically the Chinkana, because an ancient tunnel connects the two. As I have already said, more than one eyewitness I know has entered the tunnel, so it is beyond the realm of heresay or fairy tale. The question is; who made it? And why? It is possible that the basic tunnel is natural and then was later modified, by someone, but it does go, supposedly, directly from the Chinkana to the Coricancha.

The Chinkana is of course a natural stone that may have been chosen as a place to physically alter the stone because the tunnel opening was there, but the site of the Coricancha is special, and was seemingly specially placed because of its "energetic" qualities. From Inca times, and presumably back, the Coricancha was the spiritual and energetic center of the civilization. Many of the Spanish chronicles state that the Coricancha was the first building that Inca made when they entered Cusco, but as you shall see this is completely ridiculous.

5/ Coricancha

The Coricancha is perhaps the finest of all constructions in Cusco and the area. If one follows the conventional history of the migration of the Inca from the Lake Titicaca area, according to legend, the people later known as Incas began as a small group of warlike people. Manco Capac led ten Inca ayllus, or clans, from Lake Titicaca north to the fertile valley of Cusco. The Incas conquered the people of the area and took it over for themselves. They founded the city of Cusco as their capital. Manco Capac married one of his sisters to establish the royal Inca bloodline. (11)

Engineer Dan inspecting the tight stone fit of the exterior wall of the Coricancha

Okay, that is the official story, and even that which oral tradition states. However, the specific site of the Titicaca area residence of these pre-Inca (by name) is disputed; was it the Islands of the Sun and Moon, in present day Bolivia, or Tiwanaku, (also called Tiahuanaco) also in Bolivia? Based on what you have seen of the Inca style of construction we have already seen in this book, the Islands of the Sun and Moon make the most sense. My trips there have resulted in the complete lack of any Hanan Pacha or Uran Pacha styles of construction, what does exist are roughly shaped hard stone blocks fitted together with clay mortar, and adobe, filled with rough and sometimes altered field stone.

This is consistent with what I shall show you in Cusco and surroundings, and also makes sense according to the bronze chisels and stone hammers found in the archaeological record. Tiwanaku and her sister site Puma Punku are completely different, which we will get to later. The Coricancha's outer wall averages 1 meter thick, and is composed of tight fitting mortar free blocks of basalt, reputedly from a quarry 50 km away. So finely shaped are the surfaces of these stones that often a human hair will not fit in between them, through the entire 1 meter of depth. The work of bronze chisels? Impossible. Also, the western side of the Coricancha is curved, unique in the other buildings we shall see in Cusco, and the challenges to the masons who constructed it were therefore more difficult than making a straight wall.

Adding to the complication is that the eastern wall consists of almost straight, yet gently waving horizontal lines. Since the joints are so tight, one would think that the masons could have made the layers straight, even using a string as a gauge, but seemingly chose not to. Very close examination of the horizontal joint lines show tiny, but discernable bumps at the edges of the blocks, these were clearly intentional, and much more complicated to make than a flat surface. So why would they be there? Simple, the small protrusions, and corresponding recesses stop the wall rows or layers from shifting back and forth during an earthquake, because all of the mass above it would have to be lifted over the bump.

The amazing tightness of the entire Coricancha structure, however, is way beyond what is required for earthquake proofing however, it may in fact be that the builders desired that the building resonate as if it were a single stone, but this is straying into perhaps more esoteric avenues than should be entertained here.

Engineer Arlan Andrews inspecting three holes in the Coricancha wall

Dr. Arlan measuring the odd nodes that project from some of the stones

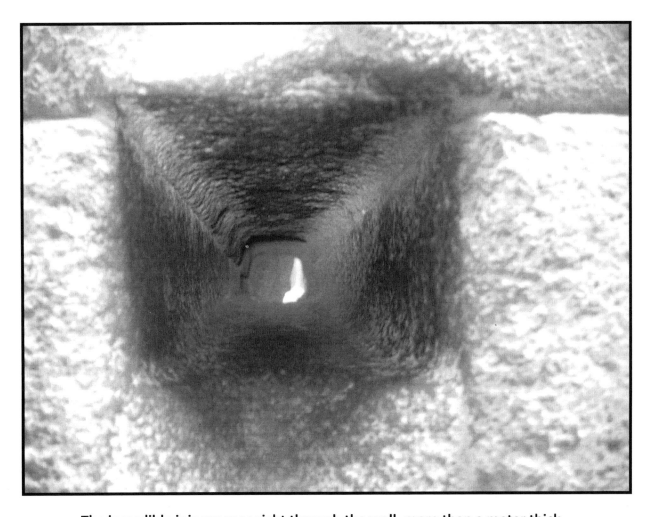

The incredible joinery goes right through the wall, more than a meter thick

The amazing fit of the stones, making the wall earthquake proof

And why the curved wall? When all other Inca period buildings tend to square or rectangular, the west side of the Coricancha has a distinct compound curve. Interestingly enough, it was Hiram Bingham III, famed for being reputedly the first non Peruvian to set eyes on Machu Picchu, who saw a direct relationship between the Temple of the Sun at Machu Picchu, and the Coricancha. In his estimation, and recounted in his book **Lost City Of The Incas**, based on his search for and discovery of the "lost" city in 1911, the Coricancha's curve was based on that of the Temple of the Sun, which was moulded to fit a natural promontory, while the Coricancha could have been made in any shape.

This intimates that aspects of Machu Picchu are older than the proposed first of the Inca buildings in Cusco and thus Machu Picchu predates Cusco, rather than the standard story that the Sapa Inca Pachacutec built the "lost" city in the 15th century AD. But more of this later.

Original curved wall of the Coricancha in the foreground

The Coricancha during the time of the Inca was, as I have said the spiritual center of the Inca, from the center of this center radiated lines, called ceque, which radiated out to all areas of the Inca world. As reported by the Spanish priest Bernabé Cobo (1582 to 1687), the ceque system broke Cuzco into four sections, corresponding to the four royal roads (and four political divisions called suyus) of the Inca. Shrines, called huacas in Quechua, were connected by the ceques, so that as you journeyed along the line, you would visit the shrines in order. Shrines located on the ceques were many things, including natural landscape features (caves, boulders, springs) and man-made features (houses, fountains, canals, palaces). The shrines had a variety of functions and meanings, related to the Inca religion, to political rulers, to family connections, to astronomical sighting points, and to land boundaries or irrigation system markers. (12)

Inside the Coricancha were a number of rectangular rooms, most believing a total of nine issuing out from the interior great wall, of which only 3 still exist. Of utmost importance was the one called the Temple of the Sun, sheeted on the interior with pure gold, and the first Inca building the Spanish demolished to the ground in 1533, immediately replacing it with the monstrous (in size) church of Santo Domingo which is still a dominant structure. The gold was of course ripped off the walls by the Spanish, "assisted" by the Inca priests whose hands were shattered if they did not work fast enough, and went to pay the ransom for Atahuallpa, last of the true Sapa Inca. His story is covered in full in my **A Brief History Of The Incas; From Rise Through Reign To Ruin**.

Recreation of what the curved wall of the Coricancha looked like

The only rooms that remain are the Temple of the Rainbow, Temple of Lightening and Temple of the Moon, which at the time of the conquest was sheeted in pure silver. That of course was ripped off the walls just as the Temple of the Sun was plundered. Gold represented the male aspect of the sun to the Inca, and silver the moon, female aspect.

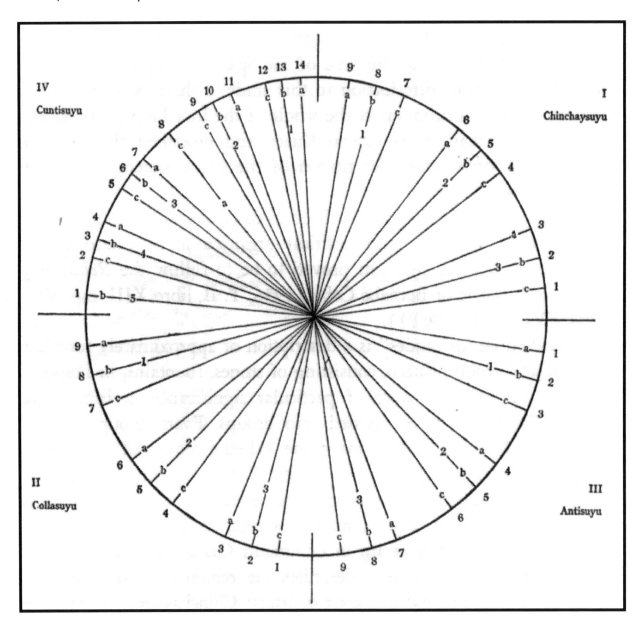

Basic layout of the ceque system; Coricancha was and is the center

These three remaining rooms are as exacting in execution as the outer wall of the Coricancha, and are so well integrated into it that all must have been made at the same time. The question is, when? Inca? No. The Inca of course named and used the rooms, and the once seemingly intact Coricancha for their own purposes, yet the evidence suggests, quite strongly, that they didn't build the structure.

We have already seen in the previous pages and examples that three cultures were responsible for the stone works, and a forth and even fifth if you include the Huari and Killka cultures. The Inca were superior to these latter two, as we shall see in proceeding examples, but it is the first two that captivate our attention; who were they, and when did they exist?

The section lower right is clearly superior to the later Inca work to the left

As a teaser to future discussion, it has been documented, and more data is confirming this, that a major catastrophe struck the planet approximately 12,000 years ago. The exact dates vary depending on the source, but most are in the range of 11,500 to 12,500 years ago, corresponding with, and resulting in the end of the last ice age, or more correctly known as the "most recent glacial period."

According to conventional science, the world's most recent glacial period began about 110,000 years ago and ended around 12,500 years ago. (13) Scientists have now been able to prove very frequent and rapid climate change, particularly at the end of what is called the Younger Dryas period, around 12,000 years ago. These fluctuations were accompanied by rapid changes in circulation in the oceans and the atmosphere. (14) During the last ice age sea level was at least 120 m lower than it is today, exposing much more area on the continents. (15)

However, the melting of the ice sheets was not likely to have been a slow and gradual process. As Graham Hancock, veteran researcher and author of such classics as **Fingerprints Of The Gods** and **Underworld** states: 'indeed most authorities would now agree that roughly half of the post-glacial meltdown was compressed into just three episodes of very rapid melting and sea-level rise – at roughly 14,000, 11,000 and 8000 years ago. Some such as Professor Shaw at the University of Alberta speak of rises "of several metres in sea-level over a matter of weeks".' (16)

What I am trying to get across here is that the end of the last "glacial period" was not a gentle affair, but rapid. A 120 m rise in global sea level would cause massive and destructive changes to the earth's environment, and thus humanity. As civilizations tend to live near bodies of water, and especially oceans, such a sea rise would tend to obviously make them flee. Also, the distribution of such an amazing amount of water, once trapped in ice at the polar regions, and then distributed around the world, could cause amazing pressure on the earth's tectonic plates, triggering earthquakes, volcanic activity etc. These could clearly alter the world's weather, and possibly the viability of life in some areas, including humans.

Some of the latest and most startling evidence of how and why the last glacial period ended comes from the work of Dr. Paul LaViolette, phycist, and relayed by this quote from Dr. Robert Schoch, geologist: 'Paul LaViolette has marshalled evidence that a major solar flare accompanied by a super solar proton event (or events) at the end of the last ice age fried the Earth (to use the description of LaViolette's hypothesis put forth in the popular Space Daily). LaViolette bases his conclusions on meticulous analyses of radiocarbon concentrations in sediment cores from the Cariaco Basin (off the coast of Venezuela) correlated with acidity spikes, high NO–3 concentrations, and rises in 10Be deposition rates in the Greenland ice record, all of which he argues are indicators of a sudden cosmic ray influx, in turn correlating with solar activity as expressed specifically through solar flares and SPEs. Additionally, there would also have been accompanying coronal mass ejections (CMEs) on an enormous scale. LaViolette dates the SPE event, which is the major focus of his 2011 paper, to "12,837 +/- 10 cal [calendar] years BP" and equates it with major faunal extinctions in North America at this time.' (17)

Schoch continues: 'In his paper LaViolette discusses some of the effects of a massive SPE and attendant solar activity for the Earth. The ozone layer, our protection from deadly UV rays, would have been greatly depleted with major ozone holes forming in some areas, that is if the ozone layer was not altogether destroyed completely! Increased doses of damaging, and potentially lethal, UV radiation could have posed a major hazard for organisms on Earth, especially in high and middle latitudes. Besides the increased UV radiation, high-energy cosmic rays that are part of a major SPE would penetrate the atmosphere and raise radiation levels on the ground. According to LaViolette's calculations, unprotected organisms at sea level during the major SPE event he studied could have accumulated radiation doses of three to six Sieverts (a unit of radiation exposure) over a period of two or three days. Lethal radiation doses for humans are in the range of about 3.5 Sieverts, and for many large mammals in the 3 to 8 Sievert range.' (18)

This would have been clearly devastating. And if this happened that long ago, ancient Cusco could have been turned into a wasteland, with the stone structures being the only witnesses that survived. Over the course of thousands of years, any human or animal traces, as well as those of plant life would be absorbed into the earth. As re-occupation occurred, the new inhabitants would most likely dwell in or near the megalithic remains, and then create their own buildings out of local organic materials such as wood.

When the Inca entered the area, again supposedly around 100 AD, oral traditions and the Spanish chronicles state, in general, three major tribes lived in the Cusco valley area. They were the Sawasiray, the Allkawisas and the Maras, who had formed an alliance that the Inca joined. (19) The Inca quickly rose to be the dominant culture, and thus we can presume that the three tribes they encountered were less socially evolved.

Curious and seemingly machined hole in the Coricancha

As the Coricancha was, from the beginning of the Inca's time in Cusco the spiritual center of the city, if we look, present day at the center of the Coricancha itself we find a curious solid stone "vessel" of some kind. Most guides in my experience do not pay particular attention to it, and don't explain what it is, how it was made, and where it came from. It, including the flared base is a solid piece of basalt stone, presumably from the same source as that use to make the Coricancha, but that is not known.

Mysterious vessel in the epicentre of the Coricancha

The amount of weathering on the surface does not allow to honestly tell if it was machined, or shaped by hand, but copper and bronze chisels could not have been responsible for it. Hewing out the interior would have been a substantial undertaking no matter what, and curious, seemingly bored holes, 5 in number can be seen. The fact that the tour guides pay little attention to this, and that the authorities of the Catholic church who oversee this, and the Coricancha as a whole have encircled it with concrete flower pots, is odd.

The 3 rooms of the interior of the Coricancha have wall which slope towards the main wall which forms the building's outline; intriguingly each one is angled at 5 degrees. The obvious reasoning for this is earthquake proofing; walls that slope in towards each other reinforce one another. The fact that this angle is consistent shows a definite building strategy, and we will see that this same 5 degrees is found in the buildings that I presume to be the oldest in Cusco.

5 degree angle of the inner walls of the Coricancha

The so called Temple of the Moon has 3 trapezoid shaped doors which allow access to its interior, however, the one in the center is not in fact a door, so what is it? Somewhat recent repairs have been conducted, though how recent is unknown; Inca or modern? The workmanship is far inferior to the original, and one can easily see tool marks, which appear to be repeated blows with small stone hammers, hence the white bruising of the stone surface.

Conventional explanation of its function, due to the presence of holes bored around the edge of the "door" was that the Inca tied and draped a tapestry there; hardly convincing to me. It remains an enigma, and is the only such "door" that I have seen anywhere.

A staircase, to the left and outside the Temple of the Moon allows you to view the top of the room, and interior. What is most intriguing is the top edge of the inner wall; it is etched with lines in succession, as well as curious circles and rectangles which protrude from the surface.

Crude but distinct etched lines on the top of the Temple of the Moon

This was first brought to my attention by Jesus Gamarra, who, upon inquiry, just shrugged as to who made these marks and what they represent. However, it seems clear that the etched lines were not made at the same time as the circular and rectangular protrusions; the latter would be far more difficult to make, and I suggest are an inherent part of the original Coricancha. They could very well have been used to track the movement of the sun, but this is a presumption on my part.

Etched lines give way to raised circles and squares

A look to the far right, and you will see the wall is broken. Returning down to the floor level, we can see that the wall is about 3 feet thick, and that the seamless joinery goes from the front all the way to the back. We can infer, but not prove that the entire Coricancha was constructed this way; a mean feat for modern builders, and impossible for the bronze chisels and stone hammers of the Inca.

If we now walk outside to the edge of the main western wall of the Coricancha we can look down on how it was constructed, because the Spanish did remove some rows. The joinery is not perfect, but very tight fitting, without mortar. Also, a short trip to the right takes us to the inside area of the main curve part of the wall. Here we see interesting protrusions, circular, square and also rectangular. These clearly had a purpose, because it would have been easier to simply make the surfaces flat.

Broken wall section on the right side of the Temple of the Moon

The theories of why these protrusions exist are varied. Most conventional archaeologists believe that they were there on purpose in order to assist in the raising of the blocks into place. A rope could be used to help pull up the block, and the protrusion would stop the rope from slipping. Interesting idea if all the blocks had such protrusions, but they don't.

When asked why some are missing, the conventional answer is that they were carved off…but why not all of them? Clearly, beings with the capacity to almost perfectly fit stone blocks together would not leave knobs sticking out of them, if only for aesthetic reasons alone.

A more "local" explanation, and that proposed by oral tradition specialists in Cusco, is that the knobs were used as solar markers, the shadows cast would, especially one presumes on important days like solstices and equinoxes, create some kind of design or point to an important point. Another, more esoteric explanation is that the projections or knobs were used to collect energy, presumably solar, to energize the building in some way. We shall see many of these knobs in other buildings later.

A few of the curious knobs found in and around Cusco

On the other side of the Coricancha, and scattered about in no particular order, are stone blocks found during excavations, and after a devastating earthquake in 1950. Many of the old Inca walls were at first thought to have been lost after the earthquake, but the granite retaining walls of the Qoricancha were exposed, as well as those of other ancient structures throughout the city. Restoration work at the Santo Domingo complex was conducted in such a way as to expose the Inca masonry formerly obscured by the super-structure without compromising the integrity of the colonial heritage. (20)

Amongst the stones are sections of the false "door" of the Temple of the Moon, as well as perhaps the most curious of all; a unique rock, broken at both ends, which has a one inch (approximately) hole bored right through it. Engineers I have shown this to, including Dan Guthrie from the UK and American veteran mechanical engineer Arlan Andrews inspected it thoroughly. Neither was able to explain how the Inca could have possibly made it, and theorized how it could have been accomplished using modern technology.

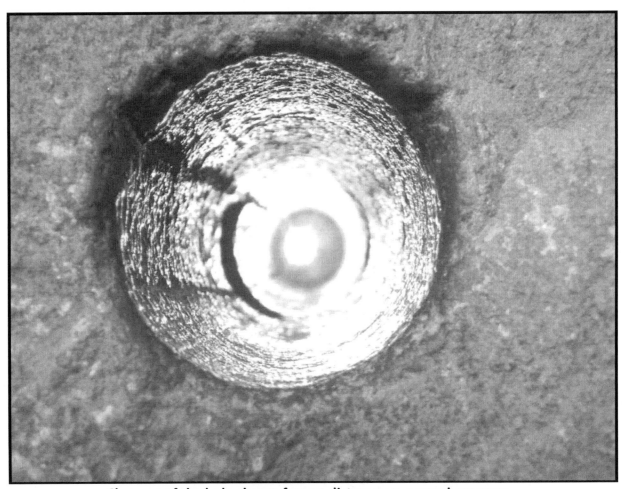

Close up of the hole shown from a distance on a previous page

The basic consensus was that some kind of circular plunge tool was used; a few spiral score marks were detected, as if it was a drill, but more interestingly perhaps are the 4 deep gouges that follow along the path that the tool took, in order to remove the material.

Similar such "core drill holes" have been found in Egypt, starting with the work of William Matthew Flinders Petrie (3 June 1853 – 28 July 1942), commonly known as Flinders Petrie, who was an English Egyptologist and a pioneer of systematic methodology in archaeology and preservation of artefacts. He found a number of drill cores in very hard stone, such as Aswan granite and quartz crystal, which are presently on display in a museum named after him at University College London, England.

Drill hole in Egypt, photo courtesy of Stephen Mehler

More recently, researchers such as Christopher Dunn, British engineer and author of **The Giza Power Plant** and **Lost Technologies Of Ancient Egypt: Lost Engineering In The Temples Of The Pharaohs** as well as Stephen Mehler and Yousef Awyan have looked, quite extensively at the evidence of ancient machining technology in Egypt, especially around the Giza plateau, and to a lesser extent Cusco, the Sacred Valley and the southern Lake Titicaca area. Chris' involvement with me in August 2012 was both illuminating and expanded this book immensely, as you shall see in the coming pages.

As we leave the Coricancha, which I am sure still holds many secrets yet to be revealed, and begin looking at the environs around it, more of ancient pre-Inca megalithic Cusco reveals itself. The name Cusco, supposedly coined by the Inca themselves translates approximately as "Navel of the World." The most common explanation for this descriptive name is that the Inca chose this site on which to build their capital, and thus center of what would become an expansive territory.

However, it could very well be that upon their first sight of the ancient megalithic remains of a once mighty and now abandoned center, they may have named it Cusco (more properly Qosqo) because this must have once been the "navel of the world." And more recently I learned that Cusco can also mean "city of stone."

Curious corner right next to the Coricancha

Just outside the front steps of the Coricancha, and towards the east, you will see a narrow street with a curious corner on the right hand side. This is one of the best examples of where we can see that three distinct builders were at work, presumably over long gaps of time in between. The lowest section, made of green andesite or granite, is megalithic. The material is only found in one other structure in Cusco, which we will get to soon. To the left is a continuation of the wall which used smaller stones of a different material, and different quarry. And on the right of the green megalithic blocks are even smaller stones, and rougher in terms of shaping. Also, that is local andesite, found all over the area, and not necessarily quarried as such.

If all of this work, in one single wall section was done during Inca times from about 1100 AD to 1532, why is it a de-evolution of knowledge and capability? Makes more sense that we are looking at vastly longer periods of time, and that what was once a megalithic wall was destroyed by a cataclysm, discovered by a later and less advanced people, and reassembled for the same or a different use.

Moving less than one block to the west, and following the Inca ceremonial route that connected the Coricancha and the Plaza de Armas, we encounter our next major examples of ancient structures. The first is in fact right in front of us, and is called the Cusicancha. Inside of it are remnants of the birthplace of the famous Sapa Inca Pachacutec, reputed builder of Machu Picchu, and greatest of the Inca territorial expansionists. He was Sapa Inca from 1438 to 1471 (22) and it is presumed that his father built the palace, as was the custom according to most historical texts.

A close look at wall in front of us, taking into account that the Spanish tore most of it down and recycled it due to the small size of the blocks shows us that tight fitting joinery is simply a façade, or veneer on the front and back. The interior is filled with clay and rubble, resulting in quite a weak structure. It is as if the Inca period builders wanted to copy the older megalithic works, but were incapable. However, they did make the building "look" as if it were a masterpiece.

As we continue west, then travel north for a block we enter a narrow street that has been there since Inca times, now called Loretto. On the left was the large walled courtyard called the Amarucancha (courtyard of the snakes) and to the right is the Acllahuasi, which was the domain of the Virgins of the Sun. They were ostensibly the "nuns" of the Coricancha's Temple of the Sun, and were thus housed nearby.

The two walls look very similar, but on close examination you will see that the wall on the right, which has a 5 degree inward sloping angle like the inner rooms of the Coricancha is of much finer construction. The horizontal lines are straighter, the stones are larger, and the joints are tighter. Also, some of the stones of the Amarucancha have the small white bruise effects that could have been made with stone hammers, while the Acllahuasi stones do not.

Another interesting point about the Acllahuasi is that the stones are "pillowed" which no one in my experience can explain as regards function. Why not simply make the surface flat? Also, some of the surfaces are shiny, and the wall itself shows distinct discolouration. The conventional answer for the latter is that air pollution from cars has caused this, but I tend to think that we may be looking at the effect of what we were exploring earlier, the devastating effect of solar plasma ejection from the sun more than 12,000 years ago.

Beautiful rounded corner of the Acclahuasi

The Amarucancha does not have the same surface effect, and thus I presume, along with the fact that it is not as well made as the Acllahuasi, to be more recent; a fine example of what the Inca could do, with their limited tool kit.

As we walk forward to the Plaza de Armas, which was the center of Cusco's activities during Inca times, we will look at our last main example of obvious megalithic pre-Inca construction. The Plaza de Armas was named by the Spanish of course, and it is where Pizarro and his men entered Cusco in 1533, coming south from Cajamarca. (23) At that time, the square was twice the size, the other half now being filled in with colonial buildings to the west, and was called Huacaypata (Place of Weeping or Meeting.) (24)

This was where the four great Inca roads met, coming from each of the cardinal directions. Walking east, along the road that once entered the Amazon jungle, we find ourselves on Hatunrumiyoq street. One block up reveals, on the right side, a green wall of polygonal shaped andesite or granite stones. This wall is part of a large courtyard, or Cancha which is named after Inca Roca, who was the Sapa Inca from 1350 to 1380.

6/ Inca Roca Wall

The author at the Inca Roca wall in Cusco

Just because the wall was named after him, does not mean that he had it made. This wall, or more properly the three walls that still exist, being the north, east and south sides are as megalithic as the Sachsayhuaman zig zag wall in terms of workmanship and style, if not grandeur. The most famous stone in all of Cusco resides here, the so called "Stone of Twelve Angles" but each of the hundreds of stones are as important as any other.

The walls have a 5 degree inward slope, though finding a flat enough surface to determine this is difficult, and each stone is unique in shape and size. They are said to be two meters thick, but no interior walls exist in their original state to properly check this, the Spanish having stuccoed the interior surfaces making them white and dull looking. A walk to the corner, and an upward gaze will show you that dark greyish black, and smaller presumably basalt stones were added to missing green polygonal stones at one time. The lack of mortar precludes this work being Spanish or Inca, so may have been a Uran Pacha repair to a Hanan Pacha wall.

Farther down the next side reveals, to those who know, that the polygonal stones were not simply fitted together, they were especially chosen and shaped to form the shapes of an Amaru (snake), a Puma and a Condor. So not only did the great builders decide to make the wall from unique stones, they also chose to create pictograms!

An oversight on my part neglected to state that this same amazing pictogram work is also found at Sachsayhuaman's zig zag wall. There, a Puma fist and fore arm, Llama, Fish and Amaru amongst other animal shapes can be detected.

Continuing down to the end of this wall, we see four distinct building styles, representing perhaps four distinct building time periods. The megalithic forms the green wall and the corner, grey presumably basalt repair work above, where one would suspect an ancient cataclysm caused earlier damage, and then, on a separate wall, we see what is classic Inca, and also colonial Spanish.

Then Inca wall is made of similar shaped andesite field stone, roughly shaped one would think using stone hammers, and the Spanish is random stones, adobe mud, straw and a somewhat flat surface of stucco mixed with white gesso.

Puma shape in the Inca Roca wall

Snake shape as well in the Inca Roca wall

Finally, as we walk down the last of the three walls, and our last site in Cusco city, we see where extensive damage to the original megalithic work seems to have happened, presumably in ancient times. One can see grooves in the stone where the Inca, or perhaps the Spanish attempted to break the great blocks, and in some cases succeeded, and other places where they attempted to put them back together again.

From Cusco we enter the Sacred Valley, taking the southern route along the Inca road. Previously we went as far as Tambo Machay, but now we move into the valley itself. There are no other known, to me at least megalithic structures until we reach Pisaq, which rises above the valley itself. As we pass the lookouts which allow us our first glimpses of the Sacred Valley, the small town of Pisaq presents itself on valley floor, nestled next to, but above the frequent flood waters of the Vilcanota, which is the sacred river (Vilca=sacred and Nota or Mayu meaning river.)

5/ Pisaq

Pisaq (which for some odd reason is named after a species of small bird) is as least as old as Inca times, though little remains as regards Inca period constructions. It is best known for its market, which tourists flock to on a daily basis.

From the last of the look outs, called Mirador in Spanish, a massive series and sets of Andene, agricultural terraces rise above the town. Careful observation shows that the Andene are arranged into the shape of a massive Condor; this is no coincidence, but was done on purpose by the presumed Inca builders. The head of the Condor faces in the direction of Machu Picchu, to the north.

View of the Condor shaped terracing of Pisaq

It is above this Condor that rests so called Inca Pisaq, a massive and sprawling complex of at least 4 levels located all over the mountain. The highest level, where the tour buses take you close to, is mainly composed of Inca period constructions, labelled by most tour guides as having been military in nature. Pisaq sits at the eastern frontier of the Sacred Valley, where it meets the Amazon highlands, and so the logic is that such a location would necessitate a check point, making sure enemies could not enter via this area.

The same has been said about Machu Picchu, that it was partly military in nature, protecting the Sacred Valley from incursions from the north, and that Ollantaytambo performed a similar function. To the west sits Choquequirao, another major mountain top site, again thought to have been partly military.

The trail to the next level, as in lower than forth leads through a gate or doorway which is megalithic and is part of an ancient wall, partially deconstructed or found in ruins during Inca times. This trail then leads through a series of stairways to the area called the Intihuatana, which is where we find an ancient "hitching post of the sun" similar to, but smaller than at Machu Picchu.

We also find that this presumed Hanan Pacha construction, again a name provided by Jesus and Alfredo Gamarra surrounded by a later Uran Pacha wall, added supposedly out of reverence for the earlier builders and their work. Also, Inca period stonework is found as well.

What confounds me and other researchers is how the "conventional" archaeologists simply label everything as having been constructed by the Inca. According to the scholar Kim MacQuarrie, Pachacuti (Pacahacutec) erected a number of royal estates to memorialize victories over other ethnic groups. Among these royal estates are Písaq (victory over the Cuyos), Ollantaytambo (victory over the Tambos) and Machu Picchu (conquest of the Vilcabamba Valley).

However, such claims are questionable. Machu Picchu was a secret place, as shown by the fact that the Spanish conquerors never found it, and there are scant, if any references that I know of concerning the existence of Pisaq prior to the arrival of said conquerors. The rather dubious wikipedia simply states "It is unknown when Inca Písac was built. Since it does not appear to have been inhabited by any pre-Inca civilization, it was most likely built no earlier than 1440." (26)

Megalithic doorway at Inca Pisaq

What we discover time and again is that Pachacutec will be listed as the builder of far more than was possible during his time, not only because the list is so long, but also because obvious signs of major works of the Hanan Pacha and Uran Pacha exist in many of these sites. In essence, the name of Pachacutec is used as the overseer and builder by many guides and scholars to fill in a void.

South of Pisaq, in the Sacred Valley there are no known major archaeological sites of significance that I know of, aside from Paucartambo, which is not actually in the valley, but somewhat off to the east. From Pisaq, the road winds upwards along the Vilcanota river all the way to the source of this sacred river, but we will get to that later.

Traveling north in the Sacred Valley, there are many Inca and pre-Inca sites, though few of any significance until one reaches Ollantaytambo. Side valleys spread out along the northern passage through the valley, and many megalithic remains may exist in them, but I have yet to explore all of them. The key to future such trips will be a dependence on local knowledge, from Quechua speaking descendants such as our great local driver Sr. Balthzar, who was born and grew up in the valley.

The one site located in a side valley about 10 km before reaching Ollantaytambo is called Naupa Iglesia. Naupa is the Quechua word for sacred, and iglesia is the Spanish word for church, quite a messy title. It is located on a very rough dirt road which leads to Cusco, and is believed to have been a major route between Cusco and the Sacred Valley during, and most likely prior to Inca times.

The ascent to Naupa Iglesia

8/ Naupa Iglesia

One approaches this site by way of Inca period stone stairs, nestled in between agricultural Andene terraces made by that culture. But what greets one at the top of the terraces, and inside a cave is truly startling. The massive boulder that you have to climb around in order to enter the cave is exquisitely carved on the other side. Some idiot, perhaps during the construction of the railway below drilled into the stone and blew the top off with dynamite, presumably thinking that Inca gold was hiding inside, which it wasn't; the stone is solid.

The "three niches" stone of Naupa Iglesia

What remains are three niches, seemingly for meditation, as they are sculpted out and seem to conform to the human back, however, this is pure speculation on my part. The central niche also has a three "stepped" pattern incorporated into it, known locally, and in Inca tradition as the "three worlds." These steps correspond to the three levels of conscious, being subconscious (represented by the snake), conscious (the Puma) and super conscious (shown as the Condor.) Whether the Inca invented this concept is not known, but it is likely that they inherited it from an older or other culture. The Inca are well known to have gleaned the finest traditions from all the cultures that they encountered and those that preceded them.

The false double door

Across and to the right of the sculpted outcrop is a carved wall with a false double door in it. The shape is rectangular, and not the trapezoid which the Inca clearly loved, and the function of this effort is inexplicable, though most guides and academics will suggest that it was a niche where a golden or stone sculpture would have been kept. However, that is quite a stretch of logic, since there are thousands of niches in solid stone as well as Inca and pre-Inca buildings which could have served such a purpose. To say that they were all used for that is the stuff of romantic and baseless nonsense.

Who made Naupa Iglesia and when? I have no clue. The workmanship would seem to be Hanan Pacha, yet there seems to evidence, in places of hand tool marks, as in stone hammers. Could the later Inca have re-shaped some of the surfaces? Possibly, but again that is moving into the realm, and too deeply, of speculation.

Close up of the central tiered niche

A carved outcrop, very similar to the "stepped" one exists at Ollantaytambo, seemingly converted during Inca times into a fountain based on the coarsely cut groove in the top by which the water moves. It has Uran Pacha constructions integrated into its sides and Ukan Pacha ones beyond that. So Naupa Iglesia has to be left for future study, and now we move on to Ollantaytambo, one of the most spectacular sites in the world.

9/ Ollantaytambo

Ollantaytambo is one of the top three archaeological sites visited in Peru, with Machu Picchu and Sachsayhuaman being the other two. However, most visitors to Ollantaytambo just touch the veneer of what is there, since it is where the train leaves for Machu Picchu, and most tourists are focused on getting to the "lost city." What they tend to see is only a small percentage of what the site has to offer.

The name itself, Ollantaytambo according to the linguist Rodolfo Cerrón Palomino is as follows. The name Ollantay comes from the Aymara ulla-nta-wi which means "place to see down", that is to say, watchtower. Tambo is Quechua meaning inn or storehouse. The testimonies of indigenous villagers, picked up by the columnist Pedro Sarmiento of Gamboa (1570), show that deep hostilities existed against the Inca, even in the tribes near to the city of Cusco. Their informants stated that Sapa Inca Pachacútec demanded to their ancestors the payment of tributes. In reprisal for the negative to obey the real orders, a powerful army attacked and it destroyed the town. Then Pachacútec claimed the area like own and it sent to build the magnificent buildings that today lasts. (27) Or so the story goes...once again Pachacutec is claimed as the great builder, or at least re-builder of this site.

It is more probable that the name comes from a person named Ollanta, who was a hero of the oral traditions of the Sacred Valley. The Ollantay Drama is considered as a classical work of Quechua literature and tells the story of a captain named Ollanta, extraneous to the Cusquenian nobility and who formed part of Inka Pachakuteq's army. He was distinguished among the others because of his bravery and great skill, but had a secret love affair with the monarch's daughter named Kusi Qoyllur. When trying to marry her officially his request was considered illegal because the rules in force forbade marriage between persons of different social status. Disappointed the young captain went deeply into Ollantaytambo and incited its population to rebellion against the imperial army, causing a war for a whole decade. He was finally captured thanks to a trick of captain Rumiñawi who appeared as having been vexed and thrown out from Qosqo and succeeded convincing Ollanta in order to get asylum; but, during the night when everyone slept he opened the city gates allowing the Qosqo army's entrance and the capture of Ollanta who was taken to the capital. Fortunately for him, when he arrived in Qosqo the Inca Pachakutec was already dead, his son being the new sovereign who was told about the true story, and with wise clemency allowed the marriage of the two lovers. (28)

Staircase and massive Andene terraces of Ollantaytambo

The name prior to this was Pacaritanpu, meaning "House Of The Dawn" or "House Of Windows." This should not be confused with the small town, near Cusco called Pacarectambo, from which erroneous stories have been written stating that it was from here that the Inca originated. In fact, Pacarectambo was not founded until after 1571, almost 40 years after the beginning of the Spanish "conquest" of the Inca. Yet, many tour guides in Cusco, and some scholars, still point to this little town as being the Inca birthplace. (29)

What is curious is that the Spanish chronicler Sarmiento (1572) who was possibly the first European to write about Pacarectambo, consulted with, according to him, 42 Quipumayoc (readers and recorders of the knotted cord system used by the Inca called quipu) who all told him the same lie! It is quite possible that they were misleading him and others, in order to save what little sacred knowledge was left of the Inca. And this included the true site of the House of the Dawn, which was Ollantaytambo. (29)

What is intriguing about it, is that it means that a place outside of Cusco, for a certain period of time, but in the vicinity, may very well have been culturally more important than the capital itself, and may in fact predate it.

For example, the Salazars, authors of the book **Cusco and the Sacred Valley of Peru** write: 'continuing along his way, Tunupa (another name for Viracochan, the great teacher who appeared soon after the Flood) arrived at a place which he called Cusco, and there he prophesized the arrival of the Incas. Then he traveled to the Sacred Valley, where he was lovingly received by the lord of Tambo. Here he left his knowledge engraved on his staff...' (30)

Another chronicler, Joan de Santa Cruz Pachacuti (1613) picks up the thread from there; ' the staff left by Viracochan (Tunupa) was transmuted to gold at the moment when one of the descendants of the Tambo lord was born. He took the name of Manco Capac and taking up the staff of gold, he directed his steps to the highest parts of a mountainous land where he founded the city of Cusco.' What Pachacuti is saying here is that the first Inca, Manco Capac, did not come from Tiwanaku, near lake Titicaca, the presumed birthplace of the Inca, but from Ollantaytambo...

In 1542, the earliest Spanish report about the origins of the Inca and Cusco, written by Vaca de Castro, from information he obtained from an Inca Quipucamayoc stated ' ...that Manco Capac, the first Inca, was the Son of the Sun and came out of a window of a house and was engendered by a ray, the splendour of the sun...then he went to the heights of a mountain where the valley of Cusco can be seen...and later founded the city.' (31)

Again from the Salazars' book we have this reference to a "window" of some kind that exists at Ollantaytambo: '...they trod upon the splendid valley of Yucay, today known as the Sacred Valley of the Incas (after having left Titicaca) and following the banks of the river that flows through it (the Willcamayu or Sacred River) they arrived at Tambo. There they entered the deep basements of the Pacaritanpu, which means "House of Dawn or House of Windows." The windows referred to seem to be the two depressions in the ground at the lower right corner of the photo. I saw them myself some months back, and they are now used as cornfields. If you look at this photo in it's entirety, you will notice that it forms the shape of a pyramid, albeit with only two sides visible. (32)

View of the pyramid shape from a nearby mountain

This intriguing "structure" is rarely if ever shown by guides to Ollantaytambo, mainly because most of them don't even know it is there! And no one, in all of the research that I have done, has a clue who made it or when. On the winter solstice of each year, June 21, the rays of the rising sun enter and strike the right one of the two windows of the pyramid. This coincides, more or less, with the celebration of the Inti Raymi, which is the Inca celebration of the rebirth of the sun, and of the history of the whole Inca civilization.

According to the Salazars' interpretation of this event and effect, 'the sun's light entering this space symbolizes the union between the Sky and the Earth, and the "illumination" of its heroes is a product of its communion, which is why they were called the Sons of the Sun.' Hence the name "House of the Dawn" has a double meaning, typical of many oral traditions; dawn as in morning, more specifically the morning of the display of the solstice, and dawn as in place and time of origins of a people; the Inca in this case. (33)

The idea that Ollantaytambo, and not Cusco was the birthplace of the Inca will shock many, but even a superficial look at the site shows that it is far older than the Inca, at least the conventional Inca timeline of about 1100 to 1533 AD. Adding more fuel to this are the writings of Fernando de Montesinos, whjo claimed to have found a "king list" of over 100 Sapa Inca rulers in succession. According to the works of Juha Hiltunen (34) 'The case of the sixth king, Manco Capac Yupanqui, is interesting. Again, in an other context I wrote about it. There are four Manco Capac's in Montesinos's king list (2nd , 6th, 61th and 77th ruler). Manco Capac Yupanqui is Manco Capac II. The name Manco Capac did bear an extraordinary halo of respect in the minds of ancient Peruvians, as did also Pachacuti. Such a names (legendary, mythohistorical characters) tend to multiply in dynastic traditions around the world.' Montesino's work therefore states that Manco Capac, the presumed first Sapa Inca who arrived in Cusco about 1100 AD was not the only one. A 77th ruler also had that name, and the center of much of the history seems to have been Ollantaytambo, and not Cusco.

The first impression of Ollantaytambo for most visitors is that the site is immense, being more than 600 hectares in size. The enormous Andene terraces that you see upon entering the gate are Inca, production being very special agricultural experiments whose seeds were shared throughout the Tahuantinsuyu as gifts to leaders that pleased the Sapa Inca. As we walk towards the staircase to the left of these Andene we pass by stones that are clearly not in their original places.

Odd shaped precision cuts are evident, and one look up and to the left shows where their original location may have been, the Temple of the Sun. Rising up the stairs, it becomes clear that the walls on the left are far more refined in construction than the Andenes to the right. They are of polygonal blocks that fit very tightly, while the Andenes are made of field stones with clay mortar in between. One could argue that the Andene were more practical than aesthetic in function, and thus were not as carefully and patiently shaped as the work on the left. However, the higher we go the more interesting it gets.

The staircase winds off to the left and up, and once we reach flat ground a number of niches present themselves, the trapezoid shapes that we have come to get used to seeing, and said by many guides to be an Inca hallmark of design. Farther along, and through the large trapezoidal gate we see inferior Inca workmanship above it, as evidenced in these old photos from the 1940s, most probably taken prior to reconstruction by the Peruvian government, since tourism here was not a major concern until at least the 1970s.

Polygonal wall below the Temple of the Sun at Ollantaytambo

Trapazoid doorway at the end of the polygonal wall

Farther up we see the first of the huge blocks, some weighing 40 tons that once made up the Temple of the Sun. We have to pause at a large andesite stone on our right and look at the side facing the valley. You can see there are what appear to be two finely crafted seats, with armrests next to each other. Of all of the so called "Inca thrones" these are perhaps the best, but what is even more interesting is where they face.

Across the valley there is a large mountain, called Pinkuylluna which bears many striking features. The most obvious are the large building across and to the right, as well as smaller ones on the far right edge. Also, to the left is another quite large structure. All are of Inca period construction as evidenced by stone mixed with mortar, though a high zoom lens or binoculars would be required to view this.

Photo from the 1940s of the "Inca Thrones"

In the center of the two main buildings, and directly facing the two chairs is a face, maybe natural, perhaps shaped or more likely a combination of both. Oral tradition calls this human profile Tunupa or Viracochan, which was the same person, whether fictitious or real no one knows.

He is said to have been a traveler who visited the Sacred Valley in ancient, most likely pre-Inca times and was a great teacher. Most accounts describe him as being tall, bearded, wearing a flowing robe and carrying a staff. Some say he had white skin, but that may be Spanish accounts, wanting some perceived "prophet" to appear European in description in order to brainwash the Native population. A very important point is to not confuse the name Viracocha with that of Viracochan.

The face of Tunupa in the center of the photo

Viracocha is the great creator god in the pre-Inca and Inca mythology in the Andes region of South America. Full name and some spelling alternatives are Wiracocha, Apu Qun Tiqsi Wiraqutra and Con-Tici (also spelled Kon-Tiki) Viracocha. Viracocha was one of the most important deities in the Inca pantheon and seen as the creator of all things, or the substance from which all things are created, and intimately associated with the sea. Viracocha created the universe, sun, moon

Close up of the face of Tunupa, also called Viracochan

and stars, time (by commanding the sun to move over the sky) and civilization itself. (35)

The face of Viracocha at Ollantaytambo can be captured as noted by Fernando and Edgar Elorrieta Salazar in their book **Cusco And The Sacred Valley Of Peru**, whereby Wiracochan is the pilgrim preacher of knowledge, the master knower of time, and described as a person with superhuman power, a tall man, with short hair, dressed like a priest or an astronomer with tunic and a bonnet with four pointed corners. (36)

There is a "crown" on top of his head, which is in fact a small sanctuary building of Inca construction, and it is still in use today as evidenced by the author who climbed there in 2010. Offerings of freshly dried coca leaves and flowers were present. By viewing from this spot down across the valley, it seems to me that his one eyed gaze is fixed on the Temple of the Condor, which we will get to in time.

Viracochan is sometimes depicted with feathers and snake like characteristics, and thus has the appearance of a plumed serpent, which is a description also given to Kukulkan of Maya oral traditions in Mexico, and also Quetzecoatl amongst the Aztec, also of Mexico.

One of many likenesses of Quetzelcoatl

Turning away from the amazing visage of Viracochan (Tunupa) and moving toward the Temple of the Sun, we have to pause at a stone on the left with a flat vertical face. It was a local guide that pointed out to engineer Dan Guthrie and me, early in 2012 that there seemed to be a cut mark in the stone, looking like a loaf of bread where the vertical slice had not completely reached the bottom, leaving the incomplete mark of the saw or other device in place.

Proposed saw cut in stone near the Temple of the Sun

The unfortunate thing was that this, said the guide, was the only example at Ollantaytambo of such a cut, and that others were at the quarry, on the other side of the valley and far up the face of the mountain. It has been well documented that the rose red granite that made up the Temple of the Sun came from this quarry, but the question has always been how was it cut, shaped and moved?

The author inspecting precision joinery at the Temple of the Sun

The conventional archaeological explanation is that teams of slaves cut the blocks and lowered them down a series of switch back trails, or pushed them over the edge, pulled the stones via ropes across or through the Vilcanota river and then dragged them up a ramp to the construction site. In general, they go on to say that the Inca made the Temple of the Sun, but never completed it for unknown reasons, hence its incomplete look.

"The Sun Temple (above) that was constructed with huge red porphyry (pink granite) boulders. The stone quarry is named Kachiqhata (Salt Slope) and is located about 4 km (2.5 miles) away on the other side of the valley, by the upper side of the opposite south-western mountains. The boulders were carved partially in the quarries, and taken down to the valley's bottom. In order to cross the river Quechuas constructed an artificial channel parallel to the natural river bed that served for deviating the river's water according to conveniences. Therefore, while

Precise 90 degree angle near the Temple of the Sun

that water flowed through one channel the other was dry, thus stones could be taken to the other side of the valley. More over, the boulders were transported to the upper spot where the temple is erected using the inclined plane that is something like a road which silhouette is clearly seen from the valley's bottom. They had the help of log rollers or rolling stones as wheels, South-American cameloids' leather ropes, levers, pulleys, and the power of hundreds and even thousands of men. Today, on the way from the quarry to the temple there are dozens of enormous stones that people know as "tired stones" because it is believed that they could never be transported to their destination; those stones are the reason why some authors claim that the Sun Temple was unfinished when the Spanish invasion happened. " (37)

Sense of scale and precision

" Scientists speculate that the masonry process might have worked like this: after carving the desired shape out of the first boulder and fitting it in place, the masons would somehow suspend the second boulder on scaffolding next to the first one. They would then have to trace out a pattern on the second boulder in order to plan the appropriate jigsaw shape that would fit the two together. In order to make a precise copy of the first boulder's edges, the masons might have used a straight stick with a hanging plum-bob to trace its edges and mark off exact points for carving on the second boulder. After tracing out the pattern, they would sculpt the stone into shape, pounding it with hand-sized stones to get the general shape before using finger-size stones for precision sanding." (38)

Pink granite block of multiple tons

According to the work of A.Hyatt and Ruth Verill, in their book **America's Ancient Civilizations** "How were such titanic blocks of stone brought to the top of the mountain from the quarries many miles away? How were they cut and fitted? How were they raised and put in place? Now one knows, no one can even guess. There are archaeologists, scientists, who would have us believe that the dense, hard andesite rock was cut, surfaced and faced by means of stone or bronze tools. Such an explanation is so utterly preposterous that it is not even worthy of serious consideration. No one ever has found anywhere any stone tool or implement that would cut or chip the andesite, and no bronze ever made will make any impression upon it." (39)

The 6 massive intact blocks of the Temple of the Sun

An American architect named Jean-Pierre Protzen attempted to replicate the fineness of the workmanship that can still be seen at the Temple of the Sun as regards the mortar less fitting of the ancient stones, with I believe less than satisfactory success using local river stones as hammers. He wrote in a Scientific American magazine article in 1886:

"It appears that the Inca technique of fitting the blocks together was based largely on trial and error. It is a laborious method, particularly if one considers the size of some of the huge stones at Sacsahuaman or Ollantaytambo. What should be kept in mind, however, is that time and labour power were probably of little concern to the Incas, who did not have a European notion of time and had plenty of tribute labour from conquered peoples at their disposal." (40)

Didn't have a European notion of time? Plenty of tribute labour from conquered peoples? What is he basing that on?

What seems more likely to me, and others who have scrutinized the Temple of the Sun and immediate area, where the so called "weary" or "tired" stones can be found, in all directions, is that a cataclysmic event happened there long before Inca times. The bronze or copper chisels that they possessed would have been useless in cutting the granite, and stone hammers would take an exorbitant amount of time to shape even the surface of the stone.

More stone shaping accuracy at Ollantaytambo

The only part of the original Temple of the Sun that remains intact is a section of one wall made up of 6 large slabs of the pink granite. In between them are thinner slabs of the same material, extremely tightly fitting. The notion that they were pounded with stone hammers to achieve this level of craftsmanship is ridiculous.

The conventional reasoning, and perhaps rightly so for the function of these shims I call them is that they were earthquake buffers. They seem fashioned to be able to move, in the event of a tremor, and absorb the shock, thereby allowing the massive blocks to stay in place. The question would be, why would the wall have to be super stable, aside from the obvious reasons of building stability?

Close up shot of the "shims" of the Temple of the Sun

The two side walls, if the original building had four sides seem to have blown out, and what remains of the opposing wall only has the lower two courses remaining. What could have allowed both of these walls to remain somewhat intact is the fact that they have hard earth behind them, whereas the side walls don't look like they did. Such a simple process would have helped to prevent the stones from being displaced.

The "tired" or "weary" stones are not in a neat pile or configuration that one might suspect would be the scene of an unfinished building project, they are literally strewn about, in all directions as if an explosion occurred from the inside, or a massive earthquake of almost unbelievable force. This, of course could have been the result of the tumultuous effects of the rapid ending of the ice age with the possibility that the earth's axis shifted in the process, from 0 degrees to our present 23.5 degrees.

There are no major megaliths that I have seen above the Temple of the Sun, though there are Inca constructions. The next major point of interest is the Temple of the Condor, which about 20 percent of people visit. But, what is perhaps as intriguing, and even fewer tourists or guides know about is the pyramid. Pyramid? Yes, it is not an actual three dimensional structure, but an optical illusion; a two dimensional construction that appears three dimensional when viewed from one specific place, called Inti Punku, which means the sun gate.

The Salazars of Cusco are the ones who best cover this topic in their **Cusco And The Sacred Valley Of Peru** book. No one as far as I can tell knows who made this, or why, but from the perspective of the Temple of the Sun the fact that this was carefully planned and executed is obvious. The simplest way to describe what you are looking at is one half of a pyramid. One edge is perpendicular to the Vilcanota river, and the opposing 180 degree edge is adjacent to the road you see right below you.

In between the two you will see is a diagonal line, which brings the two sides of the pyramid together, and you will notice the cap stone, if there ever was one, is portrayed as missing. Also, down close to the edge that borders the river you will see two fields that are conspicuously lower than the others. These seem to have been of deliberate and time consuming design, and correspond with the solsices, the sun shining directly onto one or the other depending whether it is summer or winter solstice.

Pyramid shape in the foreground, Ollantaytambo town beyond

As the Inca were regarded as the "children of the sun" and thus it is fitting that a site of initiation would be specifically designed to carry out the ritual of the new Sapa Inca to being prepared to take over from his father. If the works of Fernando de Montesinos are to be believed, this ritual could go back up to 100 plus Sapa Inca, and if their average reign was, say, 25 years, then such a ritual space could possibly have been constructed more than 2000 years before the Inca supposedly founded Cusco.

The other main place of interest in our pursuit of examples of lost ancient technologies at Ollantaytambo takes us to the Temple of the Condor, which is on the western edge of the official archaeological site. The easiest way to get there is to walk directly across the upper edge of the Andene terraces, across a well defined path from the Temple of the Sun.

Proposed Inca sun calendar

Descending the stairs, and just to the left we are presented with a large section carved into the andesite wall. Strange knob like projections are present, as well as a notch in the stone below. As far as I know there are no conventional archaeological explanations for what this is, how it was made, and who made it.

Once again, the idea that the Inca did it is highly unlikely. The oral tradition experts that I consulted state that its function was as a solstice marker, that the shadow of the sun from one of the knobs accurately enters the notch below on winter solstice, and possibly another "knob shadow" does this on summer solstice. The former was witnessed by the Salazars in their **Cusco And The Sacred Valley Of Peru** book, which documents it very well.

Many conventional scholars call the site above a "quarry"

It is around the corner from here that we see even more startling examples of stone shaping, that would have been almost impossible for the Inca to produce. As featured on the television series Ancient Aliens season 3, here we find more examples, like the ones above Cusco, of area where cubes of andesite stone appear to have been removed from the bedrock. However, at this Ollantaytambo site the removal seems to have a fresher appearance in some cases, without the heavy weathering seen at other locations.

Why this is I have no idea, and where the removed stone went I also have no answers at this time, and nor does anyone else that I know of. Many conventional archaeologists state that these are "quarries" from which the Inca extracted building materials, but have no explanation as to how this was achieved.

Moving farther along towards the Temple of the Condor, we see rougher and possibly more eroded examples of this "quarrying," with everything from cube removal to stairways that don't lead anywhere. And then, once we reach the temple, more examples appear, as well as piles of carefully shaped stones of amazing precision which were clearly once part of one or more buildings.

Scrambled remains of the Temple of the Condor

There is plenty of Inca evidence here as well, and once again the difference between what the Inca made, and that of the older megalithic builders is glaring. The reality about why the finely hewn blocks are neatly piled and lined up, and not reconstructed is because of lack of funding, or not having a clue as to how to begin a reassembly process.

The entire wall of stone in the background does make the form of a huge Condor bird, but this is more likely a work of nature than unknown hands. However, the eye of Viracochan (Tunupa) in my mind is focused directly at this area, so the same ancient builders may have been responsible for both.

Beyond this area are Inca period Andene terraces and some small examples of older work, but a 2012 trip by me through the fields that are farther along revealed no signs of anything of great interest, though a satellite image sent to me by researcher Bob Newton seemed to indicate the outlines of about 5 large manmade circles.

At this point it is time to make the interesting and well trod trip to Machu Picchu; if you keep your eyes very sharp on this one and a half hour journey, you can see the famous Inca Trail, as well as Inca structures on the other side of the Vilcanota River, as well as examples of Hanan Pacha right next to the train tracks. I get the feeling that the railway was built upon another Inca trail…

10/ Machu Picchu

Machu Picchu as seen from the famous Inca Trail

The train to Machu Picchu leaves Ollantaytambo station, and takes you to Aguas Calientes (meaning hot water) where Inca period thermal baths exist, but not much else of historical interest. Without Machu Picchu and its average of 2000 plus tourists per day, the town simply would not exist. As a tip, there is a road system that leads from Ollantaytambo to Aguas Calientes, but is somewhat more time consuming to use. The first hint of its existence is the fact that the large buses which take people from Aguas Calientes to the entrance of Machu Picchu clearly didn't come by train, since there are several tunnels along the way with very little head room!

The trip by bus from Aguas Calientes to the citedal of Machu Picchu takes about 20 minutes, and is overpriced like everything at Machu Picchu, but is expedient. After traveling through a series of "switchbacks" you reach the front gate, where, conveniently, my books await you! Machu Picchu is quite enormous in size, and there is no way you can see everything in one day. Complete books could be written about the place, but we are going to focus on the megalithic aspects. A much more detailed account is available in my book **Machu Picchu: Virtual Guide And Secrets Revealed**, again, available in Cusco, at the Machu Picchu bookstore, and as an e-book through **www.hiddenincatours.com**.

Machu Picchu means "old bird" in the Quechua language, with "machu" meaning old, and picchu being bird. Thus, a large mountain which is the backdrop to this site means "young bird" because its name is Huayna Picchu, with "huayna" being the Quechua word for young. An important new revelation to me, as of August 2012 and thanks to my Ollantaytambo based guide friend Rogelio Gibaja Tapia, is that the way most people pronounce Machu Picchu is incorrect.

According to Rogelio, whose grandparents were fluent Quechua speakers, the name is Machu Pic'chu (peek chew) and not Machu Picchu (pea chew.) The word Picchu in fact means penis, so we will respect this from now on in the book.

Now right off the bat you should also know that Machu Pic'chu is most likely not the name that the Inca called it; the term was coined by Hiram Bingham III, the American who is reputed to be the first outsider to stand there, in 1911. There are other explorers who may very well have visited the site earlier, but Bingham made it famous to the world thanks to his alma mater, Princeton University, and the National Geographic Society.

He was in the vicinity of the site and asked local people where he could see large stone structures. A local farmer told him that such things were on a nearby mountain, called Machu Pic'chu, and the farmer's son took Bingham up an ancient and vine choked trail to the site of the now famous "lost city" which funnily enough was being occupied, or the central square at least, by other farmers growing crops.

The city was largely intact, and we have photos from very soon after the discovery by Bingham that this was the case. Even these earlier depictions show us the presence of at least three distinct building styles, the Inca being the last, and crudest. However, this is not what the official guides on Machu Pic'chu will tell you. They get their official status by attending and graduating from government guide schools, and have to adhere to the strict story it says, that the Inca built everything.

Very early photo of Machu Pic'chu

In fact, on some trips I took in 2011 I was asked to leave Machu Pic'chu, because I was accused of guiding without a licence. It is not that all guides don't like what I have to say, they are protecting their "turf." Some in fact have bought my books!

Most likely 80 to 90 percent of Machu Pic'chu was constructed by the Inca during the reign of the Sapa Inca Pachacutec, but it is the other percentage that is truly revealing. All of the great terracing that you see upon entering the site is Inca, and brilliant at that, in terms of sheer volume and execution. There are enough Andene to clearly make the site self sufficient, and water was channelled in abundance for all of the needs of the 500 to perhaps 1000 people who lived there.

The function of Machu Pic'chu is one of great debate, because it is generally regarded as having been a secret place that the general public didn't know about, and hence the Spanish conquistadors never found it. According to standard knowledge, the construction of Machu Pic'chu appears to date from the period of the two great Incas, Pachacutec Inca Yupanqui (1438-71) and Tupac Inca Yupanqui (1472-93). (41) It was abandoned just over 100 years later, in 1572, as a belated

Temple of the Sun at Machu Pic'chu photographed early in the 20th century

result of the Spanish Conquest, and it is possible that most of its inhabitants died from smallpox introduced by travelers before the Spanish conquistadors arrived in the area. (42)

Most writers, based on what I don't know, say that Machu Pic'chu was a royal palace, a place for the Inca to live during the relatively cold months of the winter, because Machu Pic'chu is on the edge of the Amazon jungle, and about 2000 feet lower than Cusco in elevation. But it is more likely that it was even more important than that.

Its secrecy was more likely due to the fact that the Inca nobles needed a place to meet to discuss the affairs of state away from the prying eyes of the general public, and the warm, beautiful and spa-like atmosphere of Machu Pic'chu would have been perfect. In short, it would have been similar to today's Camp David in the United States, which is where the US President meets with dignitaries and discusses important and perhaps secret subjects in private.

By the time of Pachacutec, the Inca civilization had become quite large, and it would have been important that representatives in the south, north, east and west had a central place to meet and tell the Sapa Inca and others of the goings on in their respective districts.

The actual name of the city or citadel is, according to Jesus and Alfredo Gamarra *Yllampu* which means the "Dwelling Place Of The Gods." It is speculation on my part, but such a name may have been concocted by the Inca as a result of their discovering the site, seeing that ancient structures existed there and being in awe, thought that "gods" must have built it.

The first major example of the presence of the megalithic builders is at the Temple of the Sun, which stands out because it is rounded, whereas most of the other buildings are rectangular. It seems to be Uran Pacha in construction, on a Hanan Pacha base; the merging of the two being flawless and very aesthetic. The interior is a single slab of sculpted bedrock, with lines and grooves pointing in different directions. The only one that concerns most guides and archaeologists is that which lines up with the first ray of the sun on solstices entering through an appropriately placed Uran Pacha window opening.

It is the seemingly natural curve of the base of this Temple of the Sun which Hiram Bingham found curious, and compared it to the bulging curved wall at the Coricancha in Cusco. He theorized that since the design of the Coricancha's curves were clearly deliberate, and the Temple of the Sun at Machu Pic'chu presumably natural, that the latter preceded the former in construction. This clearly flies in the face of the thoughts, made by academics that Pachacutec was the first builder in the 15th century A.D. Underneath it is a small shaped cavern done by the Hanan Pacha builders, called a tomb by most guides, but that is not based on much of anything.

View of the interior of the Temple of the Sun from the early 20th century

Recent photo by the author of the Temple of the Sun

Shot of the chamber under the Temple of the Sun

The next place of extreme interest for us is the area around and including the Intihuatana (Hitching Post of the Sun.) We approach this area from the Temple of the Sun, and the three sided structure that presents itself is very curious, because clearly some kind of land subsidence has occurred. When this occurred is unclear, but we do see three distinct building styles, Hanan Pacha, Uran pacha and the Inca.

A massive cube block at the base, and one on either side seem to be Hanan Pacha, with smaller but finely shaped Uran Pacha stones above, and Inca tops these two. Again, because we have photographs from 100 years ago, we can see that Hiram Bingham and his crew basically found it as it stands, and the damage to the main wall probably preceded Inca occupation. The fact that the stones are so heavy probably prevented the Inca from being able to repair it.

Around the corner from here is a small room with astonishing acoustics. If you place you head inside one of these trapezoidal recesses, the reverberation volume is quite amazing. It is my belief, and those of some oral tradition experts in the area that this room was used by priests in ancient times for meditation and

Early excavations of the "three sided structure"

Old photo of the "three sided structure showing megalithic blocks

moving into an alternate state of consciousness prior to moving up the close by flights of stairs to the Intihuatana.

And this perhaps the most perplexing and most famous feature at Machu Pic'chu. The "hitching post" is called that because it is believed the Inca used it as a solstice marker, in that it seems positioned in relation to these events. However, the amount of work required to shape it, taking into account that it and almost everything else at the site is made of local white granite, to me indicates that it had far more uses than this.

It is not simply a carved rock, but is the exposed top of the mountain. If the Inca just needed a solar marker they could have made one by stacking stones and using clay as mortar, or simply used one large stone. There are so many different edges and angles carved into the Intihuatana that I am sure it had more profound

The author at the Intihuatana

functions, but what those were I have no clue as of yet. Also, it looks very much like it is Hanan Pacha in construction, and not Inca due to the weathering of the stone, and lack of tool marks. Of course "experts" will say that the Inca used sand to rub out any marks, but I doubt that.

Each of the four main corners of the Intihuatana line up with specific mountains, and supposedly the cardinal compass directions, as in north, south east and west. As well, as strange node on the side is presumed to point to magnetic north.

Intihuatana lining up with Huayna Pic'chu mountain

Members of the Chris Dunn 2012 tour with a compass

The third and last major example of megalithic pre-Inca construction is found at the Temple of the Condor, which is located across the main plaza at Machu Pic'chu. Here we find examples of Hanan Pacha, but none as spectacular as at other spots on the citadel. The curved piece of stone in front of the bedrock outline of a presumed Condor is said to represent the white ring around the mature bird's neck, but it may not be so. If you venture in this general area you will notice that Uran Pacha seems to make up the bulk of some of the walls of buildings, and then transitions into a peak which is of Inca making. What this infers is that prior to the Inca presence the buildings of the Uran, and perhaps Hanan Pacha cultures had either flat roofs, or no roofs at all. The more you look, the more it is obvious that the peaked roof concept was an Inca addition.

Condor shaped stone at the Temple of the Condor

There are no great signs of megalithic work up on Huayna Pic'chu that I could see after two trips up the 2000 stairs to the top; kudos to the Inca themselves for their masterworks here. Some guides say that the function of the quite large building near the peak was as a sentry point for military personnel with sharp eyes out for coming danger, however, it seems more likely that it was a quiet place for priests perhaps to dwell. There are enough Andene terraces here clinging to the mountainside that a small population of people could live without, perhaps, ever having to come down.

There were 2 major trails, though narrow which allowed access to Machu Pic'chu, and perhaps 3 or more minor ones. One is of course the famous Inca Trail that hundreds of paying hikers use each day, starting near Ollantaytambo, and the other is on the western edge, having an amazing drawbridge which unfortunately is out of bounds to visitors. These show that Machu Pic'chu's access could easily be restricted, and thus adds to the idea that it was a secret "Camp David" of high ranking Inca officials.

The Inti Punku (Sun Gate) an hour's walk along the Inca Trail

At the end of the main Machu Pic'chu Inca Trail, close to the so called Caretaker's Hut is an amazing shaped stone that looks like a comfortable place for a prone body to lay. It seems to be Hanan Pacha, and is improperly labelled as a "sacrificial stone." This is the same old garbage that gets spewed out and is the result, I believe, of Catholic conditioning. Very few examples of the Inca sacrificing anyone has been substantiated, and I believe such suggestions are a psychological trick and brain washing technique used by early church officials to make the Inca heirs ashamed of their ancestry; control the mind and you control the destiny of people. It could more likely have been a place of meditation star gazing or some much more civilized pursuit, but that is a guess.

The so called "Sacrificial Rock" at Machu Pic'chu

Finally, one of the most beautiful and excellent examples of the great megalithic builders in the Machu Pic'chu area is the Temple of the Moon, visited by perhaps 10 out of the 2000 plus people who go to Machu Pic'chu each day. It is located around the back of Huayna Pic'chu mountain, and takes about 2 hours of hard up and down climbing to get to. There are Inca buildings and additions to older structures here as well, and the Uran Pacha presence is perhaps the finest example of stone work at Machu Pic'chu as regards aesthetics and execution.

Terraces and outer buildings of the Temple of the Moon

Entrance to the Temple of the Moon cave

A far more detailed account of the structures in and around Machu Pic'chu is covered thoroughly in my book **Machu Picchu: Virtual Guide And Secrets** Revealed, available through various bookstores in Cusco, and as an e-book via **www.hiddenincatours.com** as well as **www.amazon.com**.

Another site in the area, but difficult to get to is Vilcabamba, or Espíritu Pampa (from Quechua: Willkapampa, "sacred valley") which was a city supposedly founded by Manco Inca in 1539 and was the last refuge of the Inca civilization until it fell to the Spaniards in 1572, signalling the end of Inca resistance to Spanish rule. However, there are fine examples of both Uran Pacha and Hanan Pacha constructions here, so it is probably several thousands of years old.

The famous "White Rock" at Espiritu Pampa

The first outsiders in modern times to rediscover the remote forest site that has since come to be identified with Old Vilcabamba (Vilcabamba la Vieja) were three men from Cusco: Manuel Ugarte, Manuel Lopez Torres, and Juan Cancio Saavedra, in 1892. In 1911, Hiram Bingham with his book Lost City of the Incas brought to public attention the site of the ruins of the city at the remote forest site then called Espíritu Pampa. Bingham, however, did not realize its significance and believed that Machu Picchu was the fabled "Vilcabamba", lost city and last refuge of the Incas.I have not yet personally visited the site, and thus can't offer much more information about it.

Back side of the "White Rock"

The other place I have not yet been, but is well worth mentioning is Choquequirao (Southern Quechua: *Chuqi K'iraw*, "Cradle of Gold" or *Choqek'iraw*) similar in structure and architecture to Machu Picchu. The ruins are buildings and terraces at levels above and below Sunch'u Pata, the truncated hill top. The hilltop was anciently levelled and ringed with stones to create a 30 by 50 m platform. (43) There appear from photos to be Hanan Pacha works here, but a thorough visit would be mandatory in order to see; the majority of the work appearing to be Inca.

The magfifcent "Sisiter City" of Machu Pic'chu called Choquequirao

Agricultural Andene of Choquequirao

From here, we are going to explore in the 4 cardinal directions from Cusco, starting with the south, and traveling along the main modern road, much of which was built on top of a major Inca trail, the Qapaq Nan, which means the "royal road."

11/ Inti Punku

The first major site of interest is the Inti Punku, or Gate of the Sun which is located about an hour's drive from Cusco. During Inca times it was the main entry point into Cusco from the south, and would have been defended by the military

Engineer Arlan Andrews inspecting the Inti Punku megaliths

to insure that enemies, as well as diseases did not enter the city. Also, it is likely that it served as a toll both, because all merchandise traveling along the Qapaq Nan was taxed.

It will seem obvious to you, now that you have looked at so many photos in this book that the Inca expanded on an earlier structure, which was of megalithic origins. As well, it is my contention that the Inca, after they had been chased out the southern Lake Titicaca area in the ninth century A.D. by the Aymara people, as covered in my **A Brief History Of The Incas** book traveled along the Qapaq Nan north, discovering these enigmatic ruins along the way.

Inca construction in the foreground and megalithic farther back

A very important point to make is that the Inca did not build this major road, nor, possibly, did they make many of them. The Wari culture (also spelled Huari) were a Middle Horizon civilization that flourished in the south-central Andes and coastal area of modern-day Peru, from about CE 500 to 1000. They greatly influenced the surrounding countryside, creating new fields with terraced field technology and investing in a major road network—both of which were used by the Inca when they began to expand their empire several centuries later. However, little is known about the details of the Wari administrative structure, as they did not appear to use a form of written record. But, the emphasis on homogeneous administrative architecture and evidence for significant social stratification suggests a complex socio-political hierarchy. (44)

Example of pre-Inca Wari construction

However, based on the fact that most major found megalithic ruins exist close to the major roads such as the Qapaq Nan obviously strongly suggests that these thoroughfares are thousands of years old. The present highway actually bypasses the ancient Qapac Nan slightly at the Inti Punku, having gone right in between the two massive walls that remain, which were heavily added to by the Inca.

The construction techniques used by the megalithic builders here appear very similar to those at the Coricancha in Cusco, seamless joinery, no mortar, and reasonably flat surfaces. Not all of the stones of the original walls are present, and could have been damaged in a major catastrophic event, or were harvested by the Inca. However the latter is unlikely, since we see that at most other sites where the Inca very carefully added their work to meld in with what was there before.

12/ Temple Of Viracocha

Next heading down the Qapaq Nan, which follows the Vilcanota River faithfully to its source and beyond, we stop at the Temple of Viracocha located close to the town of Raqchi. the Temple of Wiracocha is an enormous rectangular two-story roofed structure that measures 92 metres (302 ft) by 25.5 metres (84 ft). This structure consists of a central adobe wall some 18 to 20 meters in height with an andesite base. (45)

Prior to its destruction by the Spaniards, the temple had what is believed to be the largest single roof in the Incan Empire, having its peak at the central wall, then stretching over the columns and some 25 metres (82 ft) beyond on each side. The huge proportions of the temple, and its prominence on the site explain why the whole complex is also sometimes referred to as the Temple of Wiracocha. Or at least that is the conventional story.

The most important aspect to this place is of the presence of so much adobe. This is one of the most glaring examples of where Inca work rests on top of more sophisticated and earlier construction; the photos tell the whole story. However, most of the guides and academics insist that the Temple of Viracocha was built during the time of the Sapa (high) Inca of that name, who was the eighth Sapa Inca. His father was Yáhuar Huácac, and his son was Pachacutec. His original name was Hatun Tupaq or Ripaq; he was named after the god Viracocha after having visions of the god. (46)

What remains of the once great Temple of Viracocha

Clearly he could have had a large temple built here, but not on empty ground, as the foundation stones, and remains of round columns show us that the Uran Pacha culture was here first.

And why would, and are we finding megalithic structures so close to the Qapaq Nan, and not in other locations off in the middle of nowhere? Mainly due, I believe to the fact that the great road is very close to the Vilcanota River, and thus close to where the most productive farm land is and probably has been for thousands of years, and all great cultures were masters of agriculture, thus allowing them to have the energy and resources to have high civilizations.

Wari or Inca constructions in the area are clearly of lesser quality

13/ Pucara

Beyond the Temple of Viracocha and along the Qapaq Nan there is little obvious evidence of megalithic structures that I know of until we reach Pucara, which is near the source of the Vilcanota River. Pucara was the first regional population center in the northern Lake Titicaca Basin during the Late Formative Period (500 BC- AD 200), providing valuable insights into the origins of Andean civilization in the highlands. During its peak it covered over a square kilometre and housed thousands of bureaucrats, priests, artisans, farmers, herders, and possibly warriors. The Pucara style is identified by impressive monolithic sculptures with a variety of geometric, zoomorphic, and anthropomorphic images plus intricate, multi-colour pottery in a variety of ritual and domestic forms.

There are some very odd stone sculptures at Pucara, and much influence from the Tiwanaku culture to the south, but the archaeological site itself is off limits to visitors, since it is an active "dig" location. From photos I have seen of the site, there are no megalithic remains that stand out.

One of many somewhat crude carvings at Pucara

14/ Sillustani

From here we descend down towards Lake Titicaca and the next significant place is Sillustani, just to the north and west of the lake. Sillustani is a pre-Incan burial ground on the shores of Lake Umayo near Puno in Peru. The tombs, which are built above ground in tower-like structures called chullpa, are the vestiges of the Colla people, Aymara who were conquered by the Inca in the 15th century. The structures housed the remains of complete family groups, although they were probably limited to nobility. Many of the tombs have been dynamited by grave robbers, while others were left unfinished. (47)

One of the best preserved chullpa at Sillustani

The above is the conventional story of the site, but what I have observed is far more intriguing than that. There are two kinds of chullpa at Sillustani, dramatically different from one another. Those that conventional archaeology deems to be the earlier and more crudely built are in fact most like the later ones, while the incredibly finely crafted ones are older and very megalithic.

A cruder and more recent chullpa under reconstruction

Ancestor worship and kinship were integral parts of Aymara culture, and the huge chullpas or "chupa" at Sillustani were built to house the Aymara elite of the immediate pre-Inca and Inca period. The word was used in the 19th century and comes from the Dictionary of Ludovico Bertonio (1612). Bertonio referred to the basket burials of the semi-nomadic pastoralists as "chulpas" and actually referred to stone towers as "uta Amaya" "houses of the soul."

In fact, it is highly likely that the Aymara and Inca did use these as burial places, but that does not necessarily mean that they made them. We see not only in Peru but also in many other places that ancient structures were used by different cultures over extended periods of time, and that the uses varied. The most glaring example of this could very well be the Great Pyramid at Giza in Egypt, where Egyptologists are emphatic that it was a tomb for the Pharaoh. However, no body has ever been found, and the interior is not adorned with carvings or paintings of any kind, quite unlike other known Egyptian tombs.

The incredible precision and sterile nature of the Great Pyramid's interior makes the theories of people such as Christopher Dunn both plausible and logical; that its first use was as a power plant of some kind. At Sillustani, the pre-Aymara use of the best and oldest chullpa could have also had some kind of technological function.

The make up of the chullpa are very interesting, and "thanks" to looters we can see the internal structure of them, because none are intact now. The outer shape of finely fit and mortar free igneous stone tends to be circular and fluted, with the diameter of the top being greater than the base. Also, there is a band that goes around them close to the top, and this probably had more than a ceremonial function.

There is then a hollow space inside, and a coating of thick and very fine whitish clay, which is not the same as the nearby earthen materials. Beneath this is a domed piling of stones, which one can see if you climb inside. There is only one opening in each of the chullpa, and most guides and scholars believe that the eastern positioning of this opening relates to worshipping of the sun.

However, it could have had a more pragmatic function, but what that could have been is totally the stuff of conjecture at present. Earthquake warning or seismic release? Communication installations? What is most glaring about the chullpa are the extreme differences in construction between what I deem the oldest and finest, and those made later.

The latter are similar in form, as in usually round, but rather than being of three distinct layers, with fine masonry on the outside, they are field stone glued together with local clay mud. Conventional archaeology of course regards these as being earlier, since they are cruder, but that is the opposite of the truth. If these structures were made to emulate the form of the much more sophisticated older chullpa, and used as burial towers, then it is quite probable that the elder constructions, found abandoned and in ruin would simply have been used for the same purpose.

Interior of one of the oldest and finest chullpa

Other chullpa are found in the Lake Titicaca area as well, such as at Cutimbo, which are very similar to those at Sillusatani. Curiously, there is a small museum at Sillustani that has, amongst other artefacts, elongated skulls somewhat similar to those found in Cusco and the surrounding area. This adds to the theory that the megalith makers and elongated skull people, or at least the ancestors of those that we find, may have been the same people.

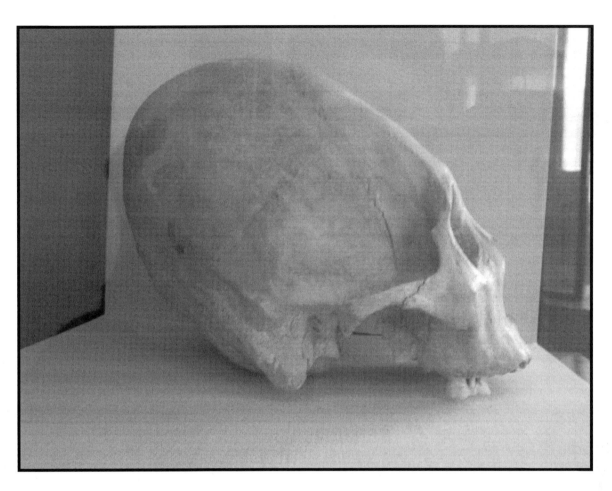

One of the elongated skulls in the Sillustani museum

15/ Chucuito

To the south of Sillustani, and on the western side of Lake Titicaca is a small archaeological site called Chucuito, within a village of the same name. Here we find a megalithic enclosure inside of which are many phallic shaped stones, presumably of basalt. The phalluses are not as finely crafted as the wall, and could be more recent. Also, there are what seem to be the remains of chullpa on the same site, but they seem to have been recycled to make other structures.

Inside the rectangular Chucuito enclosure

Chris Dunn tour inspecting the megalithic Chucuito wall

16/ Amaru Muru

Moving further south we reach a false door carved into the red sandstone which is common to the area. Called Aramu Muru or Amaru Muru, depending upon what source you reference, it is known by most locals as the "Devil's Doorway" which is a common renaming by the church of anything that pre-existed a Christian presence in the area.

Approaching the Amaru Muru "doorway"

The doorway can be found about a mile from the shores of Lake Titicaca, in a field where a sharp vertical outcropping of sand stone rises straight up out of the Altiplano. This region is in the middle of nowhere. The local inhabitants are very poor farmers and they farm the fields right in front of this doorway. They are afraid of this place and will not come near it at night, when it becomes active. There are stories of children entering into it and never returning. Strange looking beings dressed in unusual clothing have been reported walking in and out of the doorway for centuries and sometimes they headed right towards Lake Titicaca, only to disappear into the darkness. (39)

Central door with recess on either side

It was only recently "discovered" in 1996 although of course, it was already known among the Native Indians of the region. They call it the "Gate of the Gods" or "Gate to Heaven". Carved from the rock, it resembles a huge facade - some 7 metres high and some 7 metres wide - with a strange rock formation above it. In the middle of the facade there is an alcove - some 2 metres wide which one person can fit in. From a technical point of view this structure makes no sense at all. (40)

Was it made as a portal to physically travel into another world or dimension? Or is it more likely that due to the composition of the stone, being high in iron oxide, that one could and even can today communicate with others in similar "portals?" My own experiences in this recess were admittedly less than profound, but perhaps those in the past that were well trained could in fact use it as a communication device of some kind.

Scooped out vertical channels on the left and right side of the "door" are said by some "New Age" practitioners to represent the masculine and feminine aspects, but whether this is their own concocted theory, or the result of consultation with local people is unknown. Needless to say, it is a beautiful site, and the marks seemingly left behind by stone hammers indicate to me that it was made by hand, as no machine marks are evident. It is quite possible, due to its slight elevation above the present level of Lake Titicaca, that the "door" was at the shoreline of the lake several thousand years ago when Lake Titicaca was much larger in size.

17/ Tiwanaku/Puma Punku

One of the many curious stones at Puma Punku

Our next destination is Tiwanaku, or Tiahuananco, and Puma Punku, about 50 kilometres south of the Peru/Bolivia border and about 11 kilometres below the present Lake Titicaca shoreline. Its location has been touted by some authors and television personalities to virtually "in the middle of no where" however, as I just stated, it is about 11 kilometres south of the second largest lake in South America.

There is evidence that the city of Tiwanaku, or more specifically the Puma Punku area was once a port, complete with extensive docks, positioned right on the shore of Lake Titicaca. (50) The problem is that Tiahuanaco's ruins are now marooned south of the lake and more than 100 feet higher than the present shoreline. (51) Summed up very well in the stellar work by Graham Hancock, Fingerprints of the Gods, 'In the period since the city was built, it therefore follows that one of two things must have happened: either the level of lake has fallen greatly or the land on which Tiahuanaco stands has risen comparably.' (52)

Buried (until recently) ruins of Puma Punku

It does make sense that such a large and important complex like Tiwanaku would have been originally built on the shore of the lake, for the efficient movement of people and materials for example. The question of when it would have to have been originally constructed for this to be the case raises many eyebrows.

The main reason why both Tiwanaku and Puma Punku are enigmas is that, for one thing, the people who live there now, the Aymara, have only been in the area for probably 1000 or so years, driving out the Inca, who were earlier inhabitants. Or, it is probably more correct to say the proto-Inca, because it is believed that the first true Inca, Manco Capac and his sister/wife Mama Occllo, were forced to leave the area as the result of a 40 year drought.

The famous "H blocks" of Puma Punku

This fact, coupled with the somewhat worn out statement that "they had no written form of language" contributes to the fact that so little is known of either of these sites, and I do say either, because even a cursory inspection shows that they were not contemporary settlements. The one factor is the difference in stone used, and the level of craftsmanship, but the latter we will get to later. Some people are under the false assumption that Tiwanaku was built by the Inca; far from it. An excerpt from Graham Hancock's watershed masterpiece, "Fingerprints of the Gods" clues us in on this. Of the few early chronicles written by Native people soon after the conquest by the Spanish, beginning in 1532, the works of Garcilaso de la Vega stand out. His mother was a full blood royal Inca, and his father Spanish. In his great book "Royal Commentaries of the Inca," still available, in English and in paperback, he recounts what Tiwanaku (and presumably Puma Punku) looked like when viewed by someone 400 years ago:

Akapana "pyramid" which had been buried in thick mud

'We must now say something about the large and almost incredible buildings of Tiahuanaco. There is an artificial hill, of great height, built on stone foundations so that the earth will not slide. There are gigantic figures carved in stone ... these are much worn which shows their great antiquity. There are walls, the stones of which are so enormous it is difficult to imagine what human force could have put them in place. And there are the remains of strange buildings, the most remarkable being stone portals, hewn out of solid rock; these stand on bases anything up to 30 feet long, 15 feet wide and 6 feet thick, base and portal being all of one piece ... How, and with the use of what tools or implements, massive works of such size could be achieved are questions which we are unable to answer... Nor can it be imagined how such enormous stones could have been brought here ..

And Pedro Cieza de Leon, another early chronicler, of Spanish blood, who was an early visitor to Tiwanaku:

Engineer Chris Dunn making measurements of precision

'I asked the natives whether these edifices were built in the time of the Inca,' wrote the chronicler Pedro Cieza de Leon, 'They laughed at the question, affirming that they were made long before the Inca reign and ... that they had heard from their forebears that everything to be seen there appeared suddenly in the course of a single night ...'

Presumably no looting of the stones of the sights had occurred to any great degree at this time, so both of these early writers were able to see Tiwanaku and Puma Punku more or less in their undisturbed "time capsule" state. The stone used at Twanaku, at least the original structures, which were the large pillar-like obelisks, is andesite, while Puma Punku is grey diorite and red sandstone. The two sites are right next to each, and so many people regard them as being contemporary. However, the major difference in quality of workmanship most likely negates this idea. And why would mine be a preposterous notion? Many cities in Europe for example, Athens and Rome being classic examples, have the remains of buildings which date back at least 2000 years living in close proximity with ones made last year. Of course, in these cases the differences in building materials is obvious.

Massive shaped andesite slabs at Tiwanaku

According to the conventional archaeological story, the area around Tiwanaku may have been inhabited as early as 1500 BC as a small agriculturally based village. (53) Most research, though, is based around the Tiwanaku IV and V periods between AD 300 and AD 1000, during which Tiwanaku grew significantly in power. During the time period between 300 BC and AD 300 Tiwanaku is thought to have been a moral and cosmological center to which many people made pilgrimages. The ideas of cosmological prestige are the precursors to Tiwanaku's powerful empire. (54)

As for Puma Punku, a radiocarbon date was obtained by from the lowermost and oldest layer of mound fill. This layer was deposited during the first of three construction epochs and dates the initial construction of the Puma Punku at 1510 ±25 B.P. C14 (AD 440; calibrated, AD 536–600). Since the radiocarbon date came from the lowermost and oldest layer of mound fill underlying the diorite and sandstone stonework, the stonework must have been constructed sometime after 1510 ±25 B.P. C14. The excavation trenches of Vranich show that the clay, sand, and gravel fill of the Puma Punku complex lies directly on the sterile middle

Pleistocene sediments. These excavation trenches also demonstrated the lack of any so called pre-Andean Middle Horizon cultural deposits within the area of the Tiwanaku Site adjacent to the Puma Punku complex. (55)

Curious channelled andesite stone with presumed drill hole

It is theorized the Pumapunku complex as well as its surrounding temples of Tiwanaku, the Akapana pyramid, Kalasasaya, Putuni and Kerikala functioned as spiritual and ritual centers for the Tiwanaku people. This area might have been viewed as the center of the Andean world, attracting pilgrims from far away to marvel in its beauty. These structures transformed the local landscape; Puma Punku was purposely integrated with Illimani mountain, a sacred peak that the Tiwanaku possibly believed to be home to the spirits of their dead. This area was believed to have existed between heaven and Earth. The spiritual significance and the sense of wonder would have been amplified into a "mind-altering and life-changing experience." (56)

OK; but all of this is hypothetical. The last of the Tiwanaku culture is believed to have been the beginnings of the Inca, about 1000 years ago, replaced by the Aymara people, who populate the area to this day.

The quarries, from which the stone blocks used in the construction of structures at Tiwanaku came, lie at significant distances from this site. The red sandstone used in this site's structures have been determined by petrographic analysis to come from a quarry 10 kilometers away—a remarkable distance considering that the largest of these stones weighs 131 metric tons. (57) The green andesite (or some would call grey diorite) stones that were used to create the most elaborate carvings and monoliths, especially at Puma Punku originate from the Copacabana peninsula, located across Lake Titicaca, about 90 km away. One theory is that these giant andesite stones, which weigh over 40 tons were transported the some 90 kilometers across Lake Titicaca on reed boats, then laboriously dragged another 10 kilometers to the city. This I find absolutely comical, and will not bother to state the reference. 40 tons is the equivalent of more than 25 average passenger automobiles; transported by totora reed boats? And then dragged another 10 kilometers? Using what as rollers? Non existent tree trunks, or did they also fashion cylindrical stone rollers out the same material employing bronze chisels and stone hammers?

Another seemingly machined surface at Tiwanaku

Much of the architecture of the site is in a poor state of preservation, having been subjected to looting and amateur excavations attempting to locate valuables since shortly after Tiwanaku's fall; in other words, for about a thousand years both Tiwanaku and Puma Punku have been plundered. This destruction continued during the Spanish conquest and colonial period, again mainly looking for gold and stone building materials, and during 19th century and the early 20th century, and has included quarrying stone for railroad construction and target practice by military personnel. The local church in the village of Tiwanaku is one of the best examples of the looting and "recycling" of stone. How much of these sites were moved to La Paz during colonial times and later has never been fully accounted.

Puma Punku stone integrated into the local church

Puma Punku is believed to have once contained a great wharf, or so thought Arthur Posnansky, a Bolivian engineer and independent archaeologist who studied the site, as well as Tiwanaku in the 20th century, over many decades. Yet all that remains today are megalithic ruins from some cataclysmic event in history. A great earthquake? A comet that came too close to the Earth? A worldwide flood? These are all possible causes to the destruction of the once great structure that is now the ruins of Puma Punku.

Not only is there evidence to support the claim of a cataclysmic flood, but there is even evidence to support the theory that people once lived there before such a flood even occurred. The suspected flood could have happened somewhere around 12,000 years ago, and there is scientific evidence of tools, bones, and other material within flood alluvia, which suggests that a civilized people were there prior to any flood. Other evidence, that being carvings of bearded people that are not Andean, have been recorded throughout the area.

Precision shaped stone at least half buried in thick mud

In general, these bearded men are regarded as being depictions of Viracocha, the creator, or of men who were themselves called Viracocha or Viracochans.
It is highly unlikely that any of the stones in Puma Punku were cut using ancient stone cutting techniques, at least not those that we are aware of. As we have already discussed, the only tools seemingly available at the time would have been stone hammers, and perhaps a bronze chisels. The fact that bronze clasps have been found at Puma Punku means that the builders clearly had knowledge of

metallurgy, difficult to conduct at high altitude, since it is even hard to boil water at this height above sea level. But the accuracy and fine finish would be practically impossible to achieve using these tools; the stone is simply too hard, and the edges too crisp.

Well shaped andesite stone of no known function

The stones in Puma Punku are made up of granite, and diorite, and so many people speculate that diamond tools, and probably diamond power tools, which have to have been employed. Through discussions with Christopher Dunn, the engineer whom I have spoken of before, it seems that diamond tools do make sense, or carborundum (slightly softer than diamond and used in industrial applications today. The alternative idea that Chris suggests is that vibrational tools could have been used; moving at very high speed, with carborundum or diamond encrusted cutters lubricated with water, or another liquid.
Not only were these stones cut somehow, but they were finely cut. The cuts on these stones are perfectly straight. The holes cored into these stones are perfect,

and all of equal depth. How is it that these ancient people were able to cut stones like this? It is as if only master builders were allowed to come in and construct Puma Punku. All of the blocks are cut so that they interlock, and fit together like a puzzle. There is no mortar. There are only great stones that once fit together creating a structure some four levels high.

Arthur Posnansky (1873 - 1946), often called "Arturo", was at various times in his life an engineer, explorer, ship's navigator, director of a river navigation company, entrepreneur, La Paz city council member, and well known and well respected avocational archaeologist. During his lifetime, Posnansky was known as a prolific writer and researcher and for his active participation in the defence and development of Bolivia.

Multiple drill holes in a carved andesite "gate"

In 1945 (volumes I and II) and 1957 (volumes III and IV), Arthur Posnansky's final and most important book, Tihuanacu, the Cradle of American Man, was published. In it, Posnansky argued that Tiwanaku was constructed approximately 12,000 years ago by American peoples, although not by the ancestors of those then living in the area, the Aymara. Posnansky also saw Tiwanaku as the origin point of civilization throughout the Americas, including the Inca, the Maya and others.

He was of course immediately discredited by the academics of his day, and continues to be so by conventional researchers. However, his ideas, though outlandish, are based in hard science. He was a very early user of what is now the popular tool known as archaeoastronomony to date Tiwanaku, specifically the Kalasasaya.

Shattered masterpiece

The basic definition of archaeo-astronomy is, although we think our planet moves smoothly and evenly in a constant orbit, there are slight variations. It in fact has a slight wobble in its orbit, which is called precession, and this has a cycle of about

26,000 years. Also, another phenomenon, called obliquity of the ecliptic is the relationship of the angle of the earth's orbit in relation to the plane that it travels around the sun. This again is not fixed, and the axial tilt of the Earth oscillates between round 22.0°-24.6°, with a period of round 41,000 years.

Thus, the relative positions of the laid out buildings and courtyards at Tiwanaku and Puma Punku would change over time in relation to the cardinal directions of north, south, east and west. As most of the structures would have likely have been founded facing the cardinal directions, since some or all are presumed to have been made for religious purposes, the number of degrees they are off that now allows us to calculate when they would have been built.

As regards Puma Punku, and what could have happened to cause its utter destruction, Posnansky says this:

"Keystone" cuts in a multi-ton red sandstone block

"This catastrophe was caused by seismic movements which resulted in an overflow
of the waters of Lake Titicaca and in volcanic eruptions ... It is also possible that the temporary increase in the level of the lake may have been caused in part by the breaking of the bulwarks on some of the lakes further to the north and situated at a greater altitude ... thus releasing the waters which descended toward Lake Titicaca in onrushing and unrestrainable torrents....in chaotic disorder among wrought stones, utensils, tools and an endless variety
of other things. All of this has been moved, broken and accumulated in a confused heap. Anyone who would dig a trench here two metres deep could not deny that the destructive force of water, in combination with brusque movements of the earth, must have accumulated those different kinds of bones, mixing them with pottery, jewels, tools and utensils ... Layers of alluvium cover the whole field of the ruins and lacustrine sand mixed with shells from Titicaca, decomposed feldspar and volcanic ashes have accumulated in the places surrounded by walls ..."

The mournful remains of Puma Punku

Posnansky speculated that this happened about 11,000 years ago, and seems to coincide with the destructive earth changes that occurred at the end of the last Ice Age. Many theories, especially recent ones, believe that the actual melting of the great ice sheets may have happened over the course of as little as 1000 years, and the transfer of the ice into water form, and thus redistributed from solid masses near the north and south poles to being global, caused the level of the world's oceans to rise between 300 and 400 feet.

Aside from wiping any coastal dwellings and people off the map, this redistribution of weight would have been enormous pressure on the tectonic plates of the earth, causing volcanism and earthquakes of apocalyptic proportions.

Precision cut stone is scattered across many acres

Again, here we have Graham Hancock's words:

Reconstructed entrance to the Kalasasaya complex at Tiwanaku

"Thereafter, though the flood waters subsided, 'the culture of the Altiplano did not again attain a high point of development but fell rather into a total and definitive decadence'. This process was hastened by the fact that the earthquakes which had caused Lake Titicaca to engulf Tiahuanaco were only the first of many upheavals in the area. These initially resulted in the lake swelling and overflowing its banks but they soon began to have the opposite effect, slowly reducing Titicaca's depth and surface area. As the years passed, the lake continued to drain inch by inch, marooning the great city, remorselessly separating it from the waters which had previously played such a vital role in its economic life." The quote within the text is that of Posnansky.

This is in fact a viable hypothesis for what happened at Tiwanaku and Puma Punku. The devastation that would have resulted from such a catastrophe could very well have left the area lifeless for thousands of years. Not only would the people have been displaced, but the soil would have been lifted and carried away by the flood waters. Thus, nothing would grow. And also, going back to the oral traditions that were spoken of earlier, Viracocha is said to have destroyed a race of "giants" with a devastating flood back in deep antiquity. Perhaps these giants were not necessarily of giant size, but of huge mind.

For more information about Tiwanaku and Puma Punku, please consult my book: **The Enigma Of Tiwanaku And Puma Punku; A Visitor's Guide** available in e-book format via **www.hiddenincatours.com** and **www.amazon.com**.

18/ El Fuerte de Samaipata

El Fuerte at Samaipata; Inca period buildings in the foreground

El Fuerte de Samaipata (Fort Samaipata), also known simply as 'El Fuerte', is an archaeological site and UNESCO World Heritage Site located in the Santa Cruz Department, Florida Province, Bolivia. (58) It is situated in the eastern foothills of the Bolivian Andes, and is a popular tourist destination for Bolivians and foreigners alike. It is served by the nearby town of Samaipata.

It is not actually a military fortification but it is generally considered a pre-Columbian religious site, built by the Chané people, a pre-Inca culture of Arawak origin. There are also ruins of an Inca city built near the temple; the city was built during the Inca expansion to the southeast. Both Incas and Chanes suffered several raids from Guarani warriors that invaded the region from time to time. Eventually, the Guarani warriors conquered the plains and valleys of Santa Cruz and destroyed Samaipata. The Guaranis dominated the region well into the Spanish colonial period. (59)

Overview of El Fuerte with an Inca period wall in the foreground

The archaeological site of Samaipata consists of two parts: the hill with its many carvings, believed to have been the ceremonial centre of the old town (14th-16th centuries), and the area to the south of the hill, which formed the administrative and residential district. The reddish sandstone hill is divided naturally into a higher part, known as El Mirador, and a lower, where the carvings are located. The carvings in the western part include two felines on a circular base, the only examples of high-relief carving in the whole site. The remains of a stone wall of the Inca period cut across a number of the carvings, indicating a pre-Inca date. These include two parallel channels, between and alongside them there are smaller channels cut in zigzag patterns, giving rise to the local name for this feature, El Dorso de la Serpiente.

Interesting niches which are also common at ancient sites near Cusco

At the highest point is Coro de los Sacerdotes, which consists of a deeply cut circle with triangular and rectangular niches cut into its walls. Further to the east is a structure which probably represents the head of a feline. Most of the southern face of the rock was originally dominated by a series of at least five temples or sanctuaries, of which only the niches cut into their walls survive.

To be truthful, I have not yet visited this site, but will do so in the near future. The sculpted recesses and some other features show all the hallmarks of some of the ancient megalithic structures we have seen around the Cusco area, and the weathering patterns do suggest that they are of great antiquity. There are no other places of great interest south of this spot that I know of, so now we return to Cusco, and proceed in a westward direction, on the path of the megaliths.

A final shot of El Fuerte; notice the two deep "tracks" at the top

19/ Quillarumiyoq

One of the least understood, and seldom visited sites near Cusco which is quite amazing is Quillarumiyoq (or Killatumiyoq) meaning "Stones of the Moon." It is located just off a major road, built on top of a major Inca trail which leads to the Pacific coast to Paracas, home of many elongated skulls.

The intriguing "half moon" shape found at Quillarumiyoq

The main feature of Quillarumiyoq is the stone carving featured above. The name of the site is most likely based on it due to its shape, resembling a crescent moon, and also that some local experts regard it as a lunar calendar.

The angle of the arc surface suggesting a celestial function

As shown above, the angle of the surface of the arc definitely suggests that this was specifically made, out of hard andesite stone to reflect the light of either the moon, which is doubtful, or the sun, which is more likely. I was at this location with engineer Arlan Andrews in April of 2012 to test his theory that this was, and possibly still is a solar clock.

Arlan positioned himself on what he, I and his son Sean believed was the observation position and watched to see, over the course of at least 2 hours if shadows that formed on the surface of the Quillarumiyoq moved in an orderly fashion, such as a sun dial would do.

Arlan watching the shadows

It was not simply vertical shadow on the curved surface that he and I were observing, but also the angular marks in the arc above that, forming what looks like a series of seven facets. Arlan was quite convinced that his theory worked, and has since then written articles about it. I later went back at his urging some months later and took photos over the course of an hour, taking a shot every 2 minutes.

Photo taken at 11:21 am

Photo taken at 12:10 pm

Whether the above two photos conclusively shows a "solar effect" I leave up to you to decide for yourself. There are other interesting examples of stone shaping within the Quillarumiyoq archaeological area, but nothing that I have seen which is as refined as the stone displayed in the photos above. The surface of the "calendar stone" is not technically precise, but whether this is the result of weathering over extensive periods of time, or the tools used is unclear to me.

Arlan recording the Quillarumiyoq "effect"

Left side of the Quillarumiyoq stone

Cut out "step" at Quillarumiyoq

In a relatively nearby town, which is actually on the road from Cusco to Lake Titicaca, and should have been covered earlier, are two small museums which I visited with Arlan and Sean Andrews on the same day as we visited Quillarumiyoq. Andahuaylillas is a small colonial Spanish town with evidence of earlier megalithic presence with a small museum operated by Sr. Renato. In his display and also in another local museum are interesting stones which seem to have been part of an ancient water system, one presumes.

Ancient "plumbing" from the Andahuaylillas area

Bore hole through one of the Andahuaylillas stones

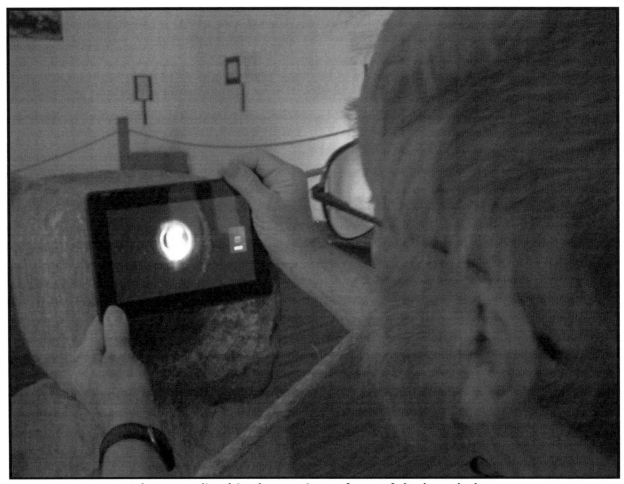
Arlan recording his observations of one of the bore holes

Arlan (paraphrasing here) seemed to think that a hand held core drill or other form of tubular metal or stone tool was used to make the holes rather than a machine, due to the irregularity of the path of that the device took. I on the other hand can not conceive of what kind of material could be found in the local area that could perform such a function. The stone that the bore holes were cut into seems to be andesite, which is between 6 and 7 on the Moh's scale of hardness, with diamond being 10.

The other thing that you find in both of these little museums is elongated skulls, thus reinforcing the idea that megalithic works and elongated heads go together, as in the people with the elongated skulls were either the ancient builders, or their ancestors were. As I hope we have clearly seen by now, the known cultures of Peru and Bolivia were not capable of constructing many of the megalithic works that we have been looking at, simply because the tools in the archaeological record would not suffice.

This in no way demeans the Inca, Wari or other cultures, NO ONE with bronze chisels and stone hammers at any time, including today could have built, for example, the Coricancha in Cusco. My favourite analogy is that since a plastic knife can not cut or shape hard wood, so a bronze chisel can not manipulate hard stone, especially not to the tolerances that we have witnessed.

The other often stated comment is the idea that a large enough work force, possibly slaves, could have achieved these majestic undertakings. However, one does have to understand that only the hands of master craftsmen could have been responsible. The same somewhat silly argument is often also cited for the construction of, for example the Great Pyramid of Giza in Egypt. Many or most of you will have seen drawings of slaves dragging a multi ton limestone block up a ramp, but hopefully few of you have been convinced that such a technique could have resulted in one of the greatest achievements in the history of our planet.

Another clue to this is the fact that for the Great Pyramid to have been constructed during the lifetime of the Pharaoh Khufu, one of these blocks, of which there are more than 2,000,000 would have had to have been placed in position every 2 minutes…

From here we travel back along the ancient Inca trail/modern road towards the Pacific Ocean. Along our way we will visit another of Arlan Andrews pet projects, Saihuite.

20/ Saihuite

One of the most amazing ancient features to be found in the Abancay department of Peru is Saihuite, also spelled Sayhuite and Saywhite. Its central feature, which few tourists visit is a sculpted stone, shown below.

The Saihuite stone in all of its glory.

Once again, conventional scholarship and local people automatically stick a "made by the Inca" sign, figuratively and literally on and near this accomplishment, and in this case it is most likely true. Hammers, especially those made out of meteoric or ? metal, or those of very hard stone such as basalt could with a lot of effort and skilled hands shape the animal figures and other patterns in this andesite stone.

The work is definitely artistic, but not of the accuracy of the brilliant megalithic works such as the Coricancha, which by the way has no animal shaped art what so ever. And this in fact brings me to an important point. Most great civilizations that we think of, such as the Sumerians, Egyptians (pharaohnic ones), Greeks and Romans were master sculptors of animal, plant and human shapes. But, the Inca were not, in my opinion.

I have seen almost no sculpture in stone that has been attributed to the Inca, which is odd. And in fact, they also were not great goldsmiths, at least not the best that Peru produced. One simply need look at the works of the Moche people of northern Peru, and to some degree the Chimu, both of which preceded the Inca to see that their work was far superior in both gold and silver than the Inca.

Moche or Chimu chicha beer vessels

And the same is true, in my opinion at least of the ceramics. Though one can hardly call the Inca works in this medium primitive, I find the earlier Moche clay accomplishments far superior.

A small selection that the Larco Museum in Lima has to offer

Anyway, just an observation, and now back to Saihuite. Numerous theories have arisen attempting to explain what the function of the Saihuite was. Among them are that it is a model of Machu Pic'chu or some other Inca city simply a work of fanciful art, or a working model of water movement.

Arlan Andrews came to Peru in April of 2012 mainly to test the idea that it was a hydrological model, created to test the flow patterns of water in the varied agricultural areas of the highlands of Peru. In order to see if this was the case, he and I, his son Sean and our trusty local driver Sr. Balthazar set out from Cusco with ladders, measuring instruments and bottles of water.

Sean, Sr. Balthazar and Arlan taking an exhaustive collection of photos

With permission from the local guard/caretaker, Arlan and Sean took an immense number of photos in order to create a three dimensional computer model of the stone, while Sr. Balthazar and I adjusted the ladders. We were very careful to never let the ladders touch the stone surface.

Then, Sean, Arlan and I took turns pouring water in different recesses and pools on the stone to see where the water would flow, always under the scrutiny and acceptance of the guard/caretaker. As it rains extensively in the area, and we were using bottled water, of course we were doing the stone no harm.

It took little time to see that Arlan's theory did indeed work.

Arlan inspecting the stone in minute detail

Depending upon which pool or recess the water was issued, it followed gravity through an immense number of different paths. We spent more than an hour at this, and were all convinced that the Saihuite stone was an engineers' hydrological model, most likely from the Inca period. And as intriguing as this stone is, it is not the only amazing megalithic thing in the immediate area.

Shaped megalithic stone that appears to have been snapped in half

The above photo is of perhaps the most striking and odd feature at Saihuite, aside from the carved stone. It is a very elaborately shaped andesite boulder, with what appear to be steps and seats. It is very similar to many of the megaliths we have seen in the Sacred Valley of Peru, but has crisper lines and finer detail than many of the others.

The strangest aspect of this particular stone is that it is broken, something that seems to have happened in the distant past due to the weathering on the broken surfaces, and also extensive lichen growth. Some may say that it was a natural fracture line that gave way, possibly during its creation, but no stone sculptor or mason would be that stupid. The solidness of the material would be the first thing that a master artisan would check for; thoroughly.

There are also channels and square as well as circular depressions in the stone surface, as the following photos show. The idea that they were for ritual purposes, such as offerings or prognostication is possible, but since we can not be definite as to what culture did the work, this is speculation at this time.

Odd depressions in the stone of unknown function

Channels and square depressions on the side of the stone

Inca period presence and works are here as well, and are quite obvious, as they are the same style of stone with mortar that we see in the walls around and in Cusco.

Inca period walls in the foreground; Saihuite stone in behind

Inca period terracing and wall complex at Saihuite

Arlan Andrews inspecting other curious stones at Saihuite

From Saihuite we head westward again along the ancient road that ends at the Pacific. There are three more sites that I wish to share with you, the first being Vilcashuaman…

21/ Vilcashuaman

Vilcashuamán (Quechua: Willkawaman, "Sacred Hawk") is the capital of Vilcas Huamán Province, Peru. It is located at an altitude of 3,490 m on the eastern slopes of the Andes. Vilcashuamán was an Inca administrative center, established after the Incas conquered the Chancas and the Pocras. According to chroniclers, Vilcashuamán was home to 40,000 people. The city was located around a large plaza where ceremonies involving sacrifices were performed. At this plaza were the city's two most important buildings: the Sun Temple (Templo del Sol) and the Ushnu, which remain to this day. It is believed that the city had the shape of a falcon, in which the Ushnu was located in the head.

The Ushnu is a truncated pyramid which is accessed through a double door jamb, characteristic of the most important compounds. In its upper platform is a large stone with unique carvings that is known as the Seat of the Inca (Asiento del Inca); it is believed to have once been covered with gold leaf.

One of Tahuantinsuyo's main administrative centres, Vilcashuaman dates back to 1100 AD. (61) However, as we start to look at some of the megalithic remains to be found here, that date should probably be pushed back extensively.

Church built on top of Inca, and possibly older remains

So called Inca double door at Vilcashuaman

The multi-tiered Ushnu

The so called Inca thrones

22/ Intihuasi

From here we continue traveling west, through the town of Ayacucho, to Incahuasi (or Incawasi) which simply means the "House of the Inca." Practically nothing is written about this site, and no information in the location itself. We met an old caretaker who gave us a basic description, that the Inca had created it as a strategic spot along the Qapaq Nan (royal road) and then it was abandoned when the Spanish arrived.

First glimpse of Intihuasi

The entrance to Intihuasi; notice the mix of stone work

As the above photo shows, someone was at Intihuasi before the Inca. Notice that, like we saw in Cusco and elsewhere the door entrance and stone to the right of it is far superior to the later Inca work. Some of the stone mixed with adobe construction may have been the result of restoration, but that is not known for sure. The story gets more interesting as we enter through this passage. The photo below shows another doorway, with a different style than the previous one, being more polygonal in style.

Another stone doorway at Intihuasi, showing polygonal construction

Though these two entryways are indeed intriguing, what I was looking for was a very specific stone, one that I had seen on the internet but could not find a good description or exact location information. However, as we advanced a little farther, and down towards a stream it showed itself to us, as seen below.

The author with the caretaker of Intihuasi, and "the" stone

"Cube" removal at Intihuasi

This was the only example of the cube-like stone removal process that is a common sight, as we have seen in the Sacred Valley area of Peru. Some conventional scholars declare this as a quarry, but why would you simply extract one block and then move on? And even more puzzling is: how would you cut it out, with what tools?

Adding to the interest was what the local caretaker showed us next, an elongated skull which he said was found at the site as seen below.

The pattern of megaliths and elongated skulls continues

The skull is part of a shrine here, inside a trapezoid niche and surrounded by offerings of fruit, water, coca leaves and tobacco. Who the "devotees" were and are I have no clue, but in fashion I also contributed to the collection. As the sun was setting, the temperature began to plummet towards zero Celsius. This place is at 3800 meters, and I still can not understand why it was chosen as a ceremonial center, or whatever it in fact was for the Inca, and the megalithic builders who came before them.

However, the next site, which is the last on our westward exploration, is in a very strategic and obvious location.

23/ Huaytara

Once again, very little is written about Huaytara, that I could find. As far as ancient structures, there appears to only be one in the small town called Huaytara, but it is an excellent example of megalithic construction. It is one of the most beautiful Inca buildings constructed in the region, and is the basis for the current Catholic Church of St. John the Baptist, built in the 16th century. (62)

View of one side of the 16th century church

This of course is written about as an Inca period building, created during the time of Sapa Inca Pachacutec, who was in power from 1438 to 1471. (63) However, if you look at the photo above, you will see three styles of building techniques used; Spanish, Inca, and "other." The lower section is clearly megalithic, that above it Inca adobe, and then Spanish colonial above that still, including the roof. It is obvious that the Spanish would use centrally located buildings like this as a church, just like they did with the Coricancha in Cusco for example. By "converting" (sorry about the pun) a sacred structure of the Inca (and earlier people) into a church, the local Native population could more easily be psychologically manipulated.

The interior of the church at Huaytara

The megalithic work here is very tight, though the interior has shown some erosion. What makes this building unique in all of Peru, and perhaps beyond are the triangular niches of the inner walls. The guide we had did not have a clue what function they had and why they were unique to this building, but my suspicion now is that they produced a special sonic quality.

One of the triangular niches of Huaytara

Immaculate corner in this megalithic building

Almost perfect alignment

The church at Huaytara is also almost perfectly aligned as regards the cardinal directions, showing that the original builders were also masters of solar alignments.

Huaytara is located in a very flat and fertile valley, with plentiful water from the Pisco River, thus it would have been an excellent place to live. Beyond this, towards the Pacific the valley narrows and the land is much drier. There are no more megalithic works beyond this point; sources of stone give way to sand and loose stone, so the architecture changes from solid rock to adobe, as can be seen here at Tambo Colorado, an Inca site.

The Inca adobe complex of Tambo Colorado

Coloured wall, hence the name Colorado, Inn of Colour

24/ Huanuco Pampa

Our final sites are to the north of Peru, beginning near the city of Huanuco, which is along the ancient Qapaq Nan route that travels northwest from Cusco. It was established there because it marked the halfway point between Cuzco and Tomebamba today in southern Ecuador. Since then the citadel has been recognized as "The Capital of Chinchaysuyo ", one of the four regions in which the call was divided politically Empire Incas. (64)

The main gate of Huanuco Pampa

All that is presumably left of the ancient megalithic works here is this gate area, as well as a large square structure. You can clearly see that to the left and right of it are inferior constructions, which one would presume to be of later manufacture. It is likely that the carved puma figures on either side of the door lintel were either carved or installed later, as their workmanship is not as good as the megalithic construction. However, having not been to this site myself, that is speculation.

The large square at Huanaco Pampa

25/ Chavin de Huantar

Chavín de Huántar is an archaeological site containing ruins and artefacts constructed beginning at least by 1200 BC until around 400-500 BC by the Chavín, a major pre-Inca culture. The site is located 250 kilometers (160 mi) north of Lima at an elevation of 3,180 meters (10,430 ft), east of the Cordillera Blanca at the start of the Conchucos Valley. (65)

Main "new temple" at Chavin; notice the mix of megalithic and stacked stones

Occupation at Chavín de Huántar has been carbon dated to at least 3000 BC, with ceremonial center activity occurring primarily toward the end of the second millennium, and through the middle of the first millennium BC. While the fairly large population was based on an agricultural economy, the city's location at the headwaters of the Marañón River, between the coast and the jungle, made it an ideal location for the dissemination and collection of both ideas and material goods. This archaeological site is a large ceremonial center that has revealed a great deal about the Chavín culture. Chavín de Huántar served as a gathering place for people of the region to come together and worship. (66)

The "new temple" of Chavin

The Old Temple, constructed early in the site's history, was an inward-facing structure composed primarily of passageways built around a circular courtyard. The structure contained obelisks and stone monuments with relief carvings depicting jaguars, caimans, and other forms with anthropomorphic features. The Lanzón Gallery, located at the very center, contained a sculpture of the Lanzón, which is assumed to be a supreme deity of Chavín de Huántar.

The "old temple at Chavin; notice the finely cut stone stairs

The New Temple, constructed between 500 and 200 BC, is also based on a gallery and plaza design and contained many relief sculptures.

The terms "old" and "new" for the temples is of course relative, but what is of interest to us here is that both seem to contain very fine and presumably ancient stone work mixed in with much cruder craftsmanship. Indeed, to my eyes at least it appears that possibly even older megalithic structures were recycled in order to construct the "old" and "new" temples.

The "entrance" to the new temple

The most obvious example of this possible recycling effort is in the above photo. The stones in the front seem completely out of place with the wall in behind, and especially the circular columns, which also appear to be made out of a different type of material. While we were visiting the site some years back, our guide told us that Japanese scientists, presumably geologists had taken samples from the columns and that the stone of which they were made is not local, and in fact they could not identify where it had come from.

Stacked wall construction of the "new" temple; notice fine hewn blocks above

The photo above also shows signs, to me at least, of the incorporation of finer shaped blocks with rough field stone. Whether this is recent reconstruction or ancient is unknown to me.

One of many subterranean corridors in the "old temple"

Under the "old temple" are a whole series of labyrinthine corridors. What their actual function was remains somewhat of a mystery. Local guides say that the acoustics of these interconnecting underground spaces create echo effects, used by the priesthood for meditative processes related to the drinking of the hallucinogenic San Pedro cactus. It would seem that many of the passages lead to the large stone Lanzon figure, a deity with human and cat like attributes.

Devotees would be led into the maze of pitch-black tunnels, eventually coming face to face with the sculpture's snarling mouth and upturned eyes. The worshipers' disorientation, in addition to the hallucinogenic effects of the San Pedro cactus they were given before entering, only heightened the visual and psychological impact of the sculpture.

The central image of the Lanzon functions as axis mundi, or pivot linking the heavens, earth and underworld. Position within the building also suggests centrality of image. (67)

The puzzling tunnels of Chavin de Huantar

The human/feline deity called the Lanzon

As we travel father, there are many examples of ancient structures and complexes which could be included in this book were the main subject megaliths. However, it isn't; what we have been looking at so far are megalithic sites that show, or intimate the presence of technological processes and traces which can't be explained within the commonly accepted archaeological theory that bronze chisels and stone hammers were the highest level of tool technology of pre-Colombian Peru and Bolivia.

Therefore, sites such as Caral, north of Lima by about 200 kilometres and a pyramidal complex at least 5000 years old, as well as the hundreds of large adobe/rock structures which line the entire Peruvian coast have not been included. There are megalithic wonders in Ecuador as well as Colombia, but this book is limited to Peru and Bolivia. So now we move on the last, and one of the oddest and least visited as well as lesser understood examples of possible "lost ancient technology;" Cumbemayo...

26/ Cumbemayo

One of the longer stone sections of Cumbemayo

Cumbe Mayo is located about 12 miles (19 km) southwest of the Peruvian city of Cajamarca, at an elevation of approximately 11,000 feet (3,300 meters). The location is best known for the ruins of a Pre-Incan aqueduct stretching approximately five miles in length. The aqueduct collected water from the Atlantic watershed and redirected it on its way to the Pacific Ocean. It is thought to have been constructed around 1500 B.C. and was once thought to be the oldest existing man-made structure in South America. The name Cumbe Mayo may be derived from a Quechua phrase, kumpi mayu, meaning "well-made water channel," or humpi mayo, meaning "thin river." (68)

The author measuring width and depth

As the above text says "it is believed" that the aqueduct could have been constructed or begun around 1500 BC, as the first known established culture, the Caxamarcha, from which the city of Cajamarca gets its name, are believed to have settled there about that time. (69) However, as these people were most likely nomadic hunter gatherers prior to this, where would their knowledge of precise stone cutting technology have come from?

And it is not "simply" the fact that the volcanic bedrock was cut and shaped to a degree of precision. At some places along the course of the aqueduct are curious zig zag patterns which are intriguing. Some opinions are that they were deliberately made in order to slow the flow of the water down in order to allow sediment to settle, while others believe that is in fact a "choke" mechanism that allows the water to in fact run uphill.

The logic behind the latter is that the zig zag would inhibit back flow of water, but a hydrological engineer should be consulted on this concept.

Detail of one of the zig zags

Another of the zig zags

The idea that these zig zags were intentionally made to go around obstructions such as boulders or stone outcrops is negated by the following photos.

The aqueduct goes straight through this rock outcrop

Detail of the short yet impressive tunnel

Another question is: why would they bother cutting such a straight path in some sections, and not in others? The aqueduct is at this time 5 miles long, but this is probably due to the silting of either end due to its having been abandoned at some point in the past. There is a section somewhat in the middle that is elevated, and seems to date from the Inca period, as it has the hall mark workmanship, in my opinion of that culture.

Cumbemayo raised aqueduct

It could have been of Spanish colonial manufacture, possibly recycled shaped stones of earlier workers, but that is speculation.

Another point of interest is that a natural stream runs alongside of much of the aqueduct, which at first would seem to have made the effort of making the artificial stone channel a waste of time. On further thought though, it could very well be that after the Cumbemayo aqueduct was abandoned, and thus not maintained as regards silt build up, that the overflowing water would follow the continues of the land, obeying gravity. Over time this water would remove enough material to create the now flowing stream. The question being; how much time?

27/ Conclusions

So what can one conclude from the contents of this book? Clearly the subject of how these ancient stone works were achieved needs to be the domain of many different disciplines; geology, archaeology, anthropology, engineering, chemistry and oral Native traditions in my mind can and do play important roles in solving the enigmas we have been looking at.

The danger in the past has been when one branch, such as archaeology decides that it alone has a monopoly on not only study, but also interpretation. Such definitely seems to have been the case in Egypt, where "Egyptologists" to a great extent have felt that they had some kind of right to monopolize all that ancient Egypt contains.

Graham Hancock has been ridiculed for his ground breaking "Fingerprints Of The Gods" for more than 15 years now; some scholars scoff at geologist Robert Schoch's observations that the Great Sphinx was weathered by water in the form of rain thousands of years before the Pharaohs ever existed. Robert Bauval has been dismissed by some for his brilliant science as regards archaeo-astronomy. Stephen Mehler has been ignored for his insights and knowledge of the oral traditions of the pre-Pharaohnic Kemetian people, taught in large part to him by his master Abdul Hakin Awyan. And Christopher Dunn, engineer has been attacked for his logical theory of the Giza Power Plant.

As you can see, many disciplines are listed in the above paragraph, with brilliant minds behind all of those endeavors. The 7,000,000,000 people of this planet deserve to know the truth of the history of where we came from as human family, in order to chart our collective future path.

Luckily for me, Peru has never been the ideological battleground that Egypt has been and still is. Archaeological research here has never had the interest or funding that other countries have had. In many ways this is a good thing, because that leaves so much yet to be shared and learned in a multi-disciplinary fashion.

The first renowned Egyptologist, William Flinders Petrie established a museum at London University. Amongst the vast collection of objects he and his team acquired were Aswan granite drill cores, as discussed earlier, and thoroughly examined by engineer Chris Dunn. So if the father of Egyptology found such artefacts fascinating, puzzling and worth examination, why shouldn't we?

Brien Foerster
Paracas Peru

28/ Bibliography

(1) http://www.mineraltown.com/infocoleccionar/mohs_scale_of_hardness.htm
(2) http://www.7wonders.org/wonders/america/peru/cusco/sacsayhuaman.aspx
(3) http://www.jstor.org/discover/10.2307/2561632?uid=2129&uid=2&uid=70&uid=4&sid=47699112055317
(4) Protzen, Jean-Pierre; Batson, Robert (1991). Inca architecture and construction at Ollantaytambo. Oxford University Press. pp. 165, 175.
(5) Gutierrez de Santa Clara 1963:252 [ca. 1600]
(6) Bauer (2007) Ancient Cuzco. University of Texas Press
(7) Bauer (2007) Ancient Cuzco. University of Texas Press
(8) Bauer (2007) Ancient Cuzco. University of Texas Press
(9) http://www.deathreference.com/Ho-Ka/Incan-Religion.html
(10) http://www.cusco.eu/view/killke-culture-of-cusco.html
(11) http://www.angelfire.com/realm/shades/nativeamericans/incaempire2.htm
(12) http://archaeology.about.com/od/cbthroughch/qt/ceque_system.htm
(13) http://geography.about.com/od/climate/a/glaciation.htm
(14) http://www.ethlife.ethz.ch/archive_articles/090216_Nature_dryas_haug/index_EN
(15) http://www.wunderground.com/climate/SeaLevelRise.asp
(16) http://www.grahamhancock.com/archive/underworld/underworld2.php?p=4
(17) http://www.dailygrail.com/Guest-Articles/2012/3/Death-Star
(18) http://www.dailygrail.com/Guest-Articles/2012/3/Death-Star
(19) Foerster, Brien (2010) A Brief History Of The Incas
(20) Koricancha Temple and Santo Domingo Convent – Cusco, Peru". Sacred-destinations.com. Retrieved 15 September 2011.

(21) Smith, Sidney (1945). "William Matthew Flinders Petrie. 1853-1942". Obituary Notices of Fellows of the Royal Society 5 (14): 3. DOI:10.1098

(22) Foerster, Brien (2010) A Brief History Of The Incas

(23) Foerster, Brien (2010) A Brief History Of The Incas

(24) Foerster, Brien (2011) Inca Footprints; A Walking Guide To Cusco And The Sacred Valley.

(25) MacQuarrie, Kim. The last Days of the Incas. Simon & Schuster. ISBN 978-0-7432-6049-7.

(26) http://en.wikipedia.org/wiki/pisac

(27) http://www.ollantaytambo.org/en/page01.php

(28) http://www.inkanegocios.com/turismo/ollantaytambo_en.html

(29) http://www.grahamhancock.com/forum/FoersterB5.php?p=2

(30) http://www.grahamhancock.com/forum/FoersterB5.php?p=3

(31) http://www.grahamhancock.com/forum/FoersterB5.php?p=3

(32) http://www.grahamhancock.com/forum/FoersterB5.php?p=4

(33) http://www.grahamhancock.com/forum/FoersterB5.php?p=4

(34) http://www.traditionalhighcultures.org/HiltunenPaper.htm

(35) Young-Sánchez, Margaret (2009). Tiwanaku: Papers from the 2005 Mayer Center Symposium at the Denver Art Museum. Denver Art Museum. ISBN 0-8061-9972-5

(36) Fernando E. Elorrieta Salazar & Edgar Elorrieta Salazar (2005) Cusco and the Sacred Valley of the Incas, pages 83-91 ISBN 978-603-45-0911-5

(37) http://www.ancientx.com/nm/anmviewer.asp?a=55

(38) http://www.ancientx.com/nm/anmviewer.asp?a=55

(39) http://www.ancientx.com/nm/anmviewer.asp?a=55

(40) http://www.ancientx.com/nm/anmviewer.asp?a=55

(41) "Historic Sanctuary of Machu Picchu". UNESCO World Heritage Centre. Retrieved 2012-05-06.

(42) McNeill, W. H.. Plagues & Peoples. p. 183.

(43) Lee, Vincent R. (1997) Inca Choqek'iraw: New Work at a Long Known Site. Cortez, CO:Sixpac Manco Publications.

(44) http://en.wikipedia.org/wiki/Wari_culture

(45)   Estadísticas de Visitantes de los Museos y Sitios Arqueológicos del Perú (1992-2008)
(46)   http://en.wikipedia.org/wiki/Viracocha_Inca
(47)   Stanish, Charles. Ancient Titicaca. University of Columbia Press. ISBN 0-520-23245-3.
(48)   http://wisp.focusphere.net/wisp/10/the-mysterious-doorway-of-amaru-muru
(49)   http://www.ancientmysteries.eu/mysteries/peru-amaru-muru/peru-amaru-muru-mystery.html
(50)   (Tiahuanacu, III, pp. 192-6. See also *Bolivia,* Lonely Planet Publications, Hawthorne, Australia, 1992, p. 156.
(51)   Harold Osborne, *Indians of the Andes: Aymaras and Quechuas,* Routledge and Kegan Paul, London, 1952, p. 55.
(52)   Hancock, Graham 1995 Three Rivers Press, a division of Crown Publishers, Inc., New York page 71.
(53)   Fagan, Brian M. The Seventy Great Mysteries of the Ancient World: Unlocking the Secrets of Past Civilizations. New York: Thames & Hudson, 2001.
(54)   Kolata, Alan L. (December 15, 1993). The Tiwanaku: Portrait of an Andean Civilization. Wiley-Blackwell. ISBN 978-1557861832.
(55)   Vranich, A., 1999, Interpreting the Meaning of Ritual Spaces: The Temple Complex of Pumapunku, Tiwanaku, Bolivia. Doctoral Dissertation, The University of Pennsylvania.
(56)   Morell, Virginia (2002). Empires Across the Andes National Geographic. Vol. 201, Iss. 6: 106
(57)   Ponce Sanginés, C. and G. M. Terrazas, 1970, Acerca De La Procedencia Del Material Lítico De Los Monumentos De Tiwanaku. Publication no. 21. Academia Nacional de Ciencias de Bolivia
(58)   http://whc.unesco.org/
(59)   El Fuerte de Samaipata." World Heritage Site. (retrieved 16 May 2011)
(60)   http://whc.unesco.org/en/list/883
(61)   http://www.easyvoyage.co.uk/peru/vilcashuaman-2795
(62)   http://www.arqueologiadelperu.com.ar/huaytara.htm

(63)	Foerster, Brien 2011 A Brief History Of The Incas: From Rise, Through Reign To Ruin Second edition Self Published.
(64)	http://es.wikipedia.org/wiki/Hu%C3%A1nuco_Pampa
(65)	http://en.wikipedia.org/wiki/Chav%C3%ADn_de_Huantar
(66)	Burger, Richard L. 2008 "Chavin de Huantar and its Sphere of Influence", In Handbook of South American Archeology, edited by H. Silverman and W. Isbell. New York: Springer, pp. 681-706.
(67)	http://en.wikipedia.org/wiki/Lanz%C3%B3n
(68)	http://en.wikipedia.org/wiki/Cumbe_Mayo
(69)	http://lavozdeltingo.blogspot.com/2010/05/la-cultura-caxamarca.html

Made in the USA
Middletown, DE
03 December 2015